Devolution

AUSTRALIA
LBC Information Services
Sydney

CANADA and USA
Carswell
Toronto—Ontario

NEW ZEALAND
Brookers
Auckland

SINGAPORE and MALAYSIA
Sweet & Maxwell Asia
Singapore and Kuala Lumpur

MODERN LEGAL STUDIES

Devolution

Professor Noreen Burrows, Ph.D

Sweet & Maxwell

London
Sweet & Maxwell
2000

Published in 2000 by
Sweet & Maxwell Limited of
100 Avenue Road London NW3 3PF
(http://www.sweetandmaxwell.co.uk)
Typeset by LBJ Typesetting Ltd of Kingsclere.
Printed in England by MPG Books Ltd, Bodmin

A CIP catalogue record for this book
is available from the British Library

ISBN 0421 72280 0

No natural forests were destroyed to make this product,
only farmed timber was used and replanted.

Contents

Table of Cases

Table of Statutes

Table of Statutory Instruments

Introduction

"The central theme of this book is that devolution, as well as being the most profound constitutional issue of the day, is likely to have more profound effects upon the workings of British politics than any other institutional reform since the war."[1] These were the opening words of Bogdanor's classic work on devolution in 1979. However, the legislation enacted in the 1970s never came into force because of lack of popular support in both Scotland and Wales. In Northern Ireland devolution was brought to an end in 1972 and direct rule imposed as a result of a sustained period of violence. Thereafter Northern Ireland was effectively governed by the Secretary of State for Northern Ireland.

More than 20 years later, it can now be asserted that devolution is indeed one of the most interesting and important processes in United Kingdom legal, constitutional and political life. This book attempts to explain some of the legal issues that have arisen as part of the process of introducing devolution into United Kingdom constitutional law. It is based on the assumption that an understanding of devolution as a process requires an attempt to compare what is happening in the three regions of Scotland, Wales and Northern Ireland.

Devolution essentially means the transfer and subsequent sharing of powers between institutions of government within a limited framework set out in legislation. As part of a New Labour agenda, it is also part of the process of modernisation of the United Kingdom constitution. In this context modernisation encompasses ideas of partnership, inclusiveness, accountability, clean politics, equality, and bringing government closer to the people. It is therefore an ambitious programme of reform. It provides an opportunity for individuals to question the existing structures of government and to evaluate the role of government in the life of their community whether this is at the local, regional, national or international level. Devolution adds a further layer of government into what is already a multi-layered legal and political society. Because devolution is uneven in the three regions, it also creates a multi-textured state.

---

[1] V. Bogdanor, *Devolution* (Oxford: OUP, 1979) 1.

1

Devolution is a process not an event.[2] It can be seen as a sequence of legal and political events. The main focus in this book is on the legal events involved in setting the process of devolution in train. However, these legal events, namely the passing of primary and secondary legislation and the recognition of new constitutional conventions and practices, cannot be seen outside a particular historical and political context. Devolution is only one of the possible variations that might have been pursued in the process of modernisation. For example, federalism or confederalism might have provided alternative models to the devolution settlement. A more radical vision might be based on a break up of the United Kingdom itself into its pre-union constituent parts. These alternatives were not seriously considered by New Labour whose constitutional reform in this respect at least is firmly rooted in previous models.

Devolution is a paradise for lawyers. In a country whose constitutional mantra is that there is no written constitution, the deference to the written word in the devolution process is astonishing. The written text is at the heart of the process. The three key Acts of the United Kingdom Parliament enacted in 1998; the Scotland Act, the Government of Wales Act and the Northern Ireland Act obviously form the centre piece of the devolution process but, in addition, there is a mass of secondary legislation adopted under those Acts. Much of the secondary legislation is as detailed and as complex as the primary legislation. In addition there are a number of written codes of practice as well as written conventions governing the relationships between the devolved institutions and the institutions of the United Kingdom. In the latter context there are concordats, agency agreements and working level agreements. The legislation may provide the big picture but the attention to detail in the additional texts suggests that little will be left to chance and that the play of politics and politicians is limited by the written word. This suggests that, at least in these early stages, devolution is a carefully controlled process. Devolution has only partially, therefore, brought about a decentralisation of power.

It can be argued that, taken together, these written texts are now the constituent acts of a *union kingdom* in which the identity and existence of the other, smaller and non-English parts of the United

---

[2] Ron Davies is credited with the phrase "devolution is a process not an event". His account of devolution in Wales is given a similar title, *Devolution: A process not an event* (Institute of Welsh Affairs, 1999).

2

Kingdom is acknowledged. The concept of the union state, as applied to the United Kingdom, recognises the differences between the constituent parts of the United Kingdom and allows distinct institutions to operate. According to Keating and Elcock "the union state reading of the constitution [was] familiar up to the late nineteenth century". According to them the development of national party politics and the uniformity imposed by the development of the welfare state in the twentieth century accounted for the decline in union state thinking.[3] Devolution is thus a return to an older constitutional view. Whether devolution can now succeed against the continuation of party politics and the continued welfare state thinking is, of course yet to be determined. The success of devolution in the long term might require a restructuring of politics and political parties and the recognition that welfare policies can be developed at different levels and paces within the United Kingdom. The break up of political parties into regional structures might be both possible and desirable. The break up of the welfare state is unlikely to have popular support. In these circumstances, the impact of devolution might, in the longer term, prove to have little real impact. Who can tell?

The most striking feature of the three Acts of Parliament enacted in 1998[4] is the extent of the differences between the devolution settlements for Scotland, Wales and Northern Ireland. In a United Kingdom context, it can be argued that such extensive differences are both useful and desirable particularly in these early days of devolution. The imposition from the centre of a uniform template for devolution would have created insurmountable political obstacles for the Labour government as it attempted to get its constitutional reform through parliament in as short a time period as possible. There are some common or shared features in the different devolution settlements. The essential structure of the institutions with an elected chamber and a cabinet style of government follows a similar same pattern, however this similarity masks the very different functional differences between the institutions and the manner in which they operate. By comparing certain aspects of the devolution

---

[3] H. Elcock and M. Keating, *Remaking the Union* (Frank Cass, 1998) 3. See also J. Mitchell, *Strategies for self government: the campaign for a Scottish Parliament* (Polygon, 1996).
[4] The Government of Wales Act, c.38, the Scotland Act, c.46, and the Northern Ireland Act, c.47.

settlements, this book seeks to explore the degree of difference or assmetry between the regional governments of the United Kingdom.[5]

By necessity, devolution was achieved in the United Kingdom by the enactment of Acts of the United Kingdom parliament. Practical and pragmatic reasons led to the adoption of three separate Acts. This compartmentalisation means that certain features of devolution are incomplete or are missing from the legislation. In particular, constitutional principles and arrangements governing the relationships between the newly created institutions themselves and between Westminster, Whitehall and the devolved administrations are lacking. These gaps are in the process of being filled by the adoption of non-legally binding mechanisms and procedures and new constitutional conventions. These principles and arrangements are designed to allow for the co-ordination of policy and to facilitate dialogue between regional and central government and by departments of government. These arrangements are enshrined in documents, some of which are excessively detailed. The use of agreements is intended to forestall political disputes but, given their structure, with control apparently being retained in the hands of Ministers of the Crown, there must also be the suspicion that arrangements which seek to co-ordinate policy may have the effect of controlling or limiting the freedom of action of the devolved institutions.

Where agreement cannot be reached by political processes the courts will inevitably be drawn into political controversies. The Judicial Committee of the Privy Council appears to have been given a central role in the resolution of devolution disputes. However, devolution issues will arise in a variety of court proceedings bringing many lower level courts into constitutional debates. This is not a new constitutional phenomenon. It has already occurred because of the interaction between national and European issues in the courts of the United Kingdom. The courts will need principles to guide them in devolution disputes. On questions relating to the relationship between national and European law the courts have been able to turn for assistance to the European Court of Justice as a higher authority

---

[5] In this book I have chosen to use the term region to describe the constituent parts of the United Kingdom. In Scotland, the term "sub-national" unit is deemed by some to be insulting. I have also avoided the use of the term "nation" because confusion may arise in discussion of the relationship between national (United Kingdom) law and European law. The book does not engage in the debate about the nature of identity politics in this context. The use of the term "region" is accepted at the European level, as in the Committee of the Regions, and this practice is followed here.

capable of giving authoritative rulings to be applied to disputes before them. The Judicial Committee will need to play a role similar to that of the European Court of Justice and will probably need to be equally as creative.

It is entirely possible that the Judicial Committee will adopt constitutional principles that are unique to the United Kingdom. It might draw on principles from the Commonwealth or from the United States. However, this book argues that valuable lessons can be drawn from European law in the resolution of disputes concerning competencies. The European Union and its Member States operate in a plural and multi-layered legal order where rules are made and administered at different levels of government. There is no written constitution governing these relationships. In order to avoid conflicts between these legal orders the European Union has had to develop constitutional principles based on an understanding of the objectives of the treaties to protect both the European Union itself and the prerogatives of the Member States. Asymmetry is an increasingly important feature of the European Union legal order as the inclusion of the principle of flexibility in the Amsterdam Treaty demonstrates. To avoid over-centralisation and to respect the autonomy of the Member States other principles have been needed. Subsidiarity has been a useful, if only partially developed, concept that can help in regulating how powers should be exercised in those difficult areas where powers are shared between different levels of government. These and other European principles might be adapted to multi-layered government in the United Kingdom in cases of disputes over devolution issues.

The devolution process has been in this first phase largely a question of institution building. The new institutions share some common features with existing United Kingdom institutions but it is striking that an attempt has been made to avoid a mere replication of Westminster. Nowhere is this more obvious than in the principles that are to inform the working of the devolved institutions. Equal opportunities, inclusiveness, and openness are not principles that are readily associated with the workings of the United Kingdom parliament and government. Yet these are the principles that it is hoped will guide the devolution settlement. It is here that the modernisation programme of New Labour does attempt to provide a principled constitutional law and the basis of a new constitutional language. Whether it delivers on these principles is yet to be seen but the ideas have been planted and, to some extent, legislated for. These ideas and principles are, therefore, worthy of serious study by lawyers.

In the chapters that follow, this book examines devolution in the light of the ideas outlined above. Chapter 1 examines New Labour's approach to devolution and its switch from being the party of centralised state control to a party that espouses devolution as part of its programme of modernisation. Chapter 2 compares the "parliamentary" institutions and analyses differences in composition between the Scottish Parliament, the National Assembly for Wales and the Northern Ireland Assembly[6]. There is a marked degree of similarity between these institutions in terms of formal structures so that it is entirely possible that there may be a great deal of convergence between them at a later date. However, in terms of functions there is a marked degree of asymmetry and these issues are explored in Chapter 3. Here the National Assembly for Wales appears to be the "odd man out" since it is not a parliament in the true sense of the word and does not have powers to adopt primary legislation. Chapter 4 compares the structure and functions of the executive or cabinet branch of government. In all three settlements there is a "cabinet style" approach reminiscent of the Westminster model. This was not the model originally envisaged for the Welsh Assembly precisely because of the differences in functions attributed to the "parliamentary" institutions. Chapter 5 deals with issues of policy formulation and policy co-ordination within the United Kingdom. The legislation is silent on these issues and so there is a need to examine the extra-legal mechanisms that operate by way of concordats and inter-ministerial and inter-departmental agreements. The special case of Northern Ireland also brings into play the role of another independent actor, the Republic of Ireland. This chapter therefore examines the role of cross-border institutions in policy formulation and policy co-ordination. Chapter 6 deals with devolution issues and how these issues are to be resolved. The focus of this chapter is on the courts. Devolution has created a vastly complex legal chess game in which the law officers have been given new roles and the courts new constitutional tasks.

---

[6] The (New) Northern Ireland Assembly was elected under the Northern Ireland (Elections) Act 1998, c.12 as a shadow Assembly. It did not have legislative or executive powers. Its purpose was to make preparations for the functioning of the fully-fledged Assembly. After devolution took place the Assembly assumed powers and it is now known as the Northern Ireland Assembly. The Assembly was suspended by the Northern Ireland Act 2000, c.1. During suspension, neither the Assembly not any of its committees was to meet, no Act could be passed by the Assembly, and no Minister was to continue to hold office.

This book does not lay claim to be a definitive work on devolution. Apart from anything else, the process of devolving power is not complete. The book was started in October 1998. By October 1999, matters in Northern Ireland appeared to have reached an impasse. Senator George Mitchell was engaged in talks between the parties to attempt to resolve the question of whether decommissioning of weapons was a prior condition of devolution. In December 1999 a break through was achieved and power was transferred to Northern Ireland. The devolved institutions were subsequently suspended after a matter of weeks by an Act of the United Kingdom Parliament on February 10, 2000. Devolution was restored in May 2000.[7]

Any European lawyer who comes to examine the process of devolution is bound to be influenced by the discipline in which he/ she normally works. Whilst there are many aspects of the European constitution which are as yet undeveloped and around which debate still rages, European Union constitutional law provides some possible approaches to solving problems of the division of powers within a multi-layered political order. One obvious common point of departure is the entire notion of process. European integration is most often theorised in terms of process of which the ultimate goal is contested. Progress is achieved in a series of political bargains whereby the objectives of integration shift reflecting the priorities of the Member States.[8] In this changing political landscape constitutional law and principles have developed over time. Devolution is similarly a process where the ultimate goal is not clear. Whether devolution will ultimately lead to a federal United Kingdom, whether further powers will be decentralised, whether parts of the United Kingdom use devolution as a spring-board to independence are questions which will be resolved over time.

Another obvious point of comparison is that neither the United Kingdom nor the European Union operates within the context of a written constitution. There are written texts, for the European Union treaties and for the United Kingdom Acts of Parliament, which provide a framework constitutional structure. In neither case are

---

[7] S.I. 2000/1445 The Northern Ireland Act 2000 (Restoration of Devolved Government) Order 2000.

[8] For example see, A. Moravscik, *The Choice for Europe* (London: UCL Press, 1998) chapter 1 for a discussion of theorising European integration. See also P. Craig, "The Nature of the Community: Integration, Democracy and Legitimacy" in P. Craig and G. De Burca (eds) *The Evolution of E.U. Law* ((Oxford: OUP, 1999) for a public lawyer's critique of this theorising.

these legal texts equivalent to a written constitution so that ambiguities in the constitutional architecture itself are left to be resolved by a combination of legal and political processes. The possibility of change and renewal is therefore ever present.

In many instances in this book there are references to European principles. European solutions are sometimes presented as possible methods of dealing with problems that have arisen or will arise in the process of devolution. At other times Europe is chosen as the point of comparison. It is suggested that this approach can assist in understanding some aspects of multi-layered governance. It is not suggested that European constitutional law is in any sense an ideal model. It is a model, however, that has the benefit of being familiar to lawyers and students in the United Kingdom precisely because of their need to understand United Kingdom constitutional law in the context of membership of the European Union. The discussion of European constitutional principles is intended to stimulate debate about the possible approaches that might be taken as the process of devolution unfolds within the United Kingdom.

Chapter 1.

New Labour and Devolution

New Labour did not invent devolution although it could be argued that it re-invented devolution as part of a policy of re-inventing itself. Devolution (although the word itself is used only in the twentieth century) was the leitmotif of the nineteenth and twentieth centuries rather than the herald of the twenty-first. For a large part of its existence the United Kingdom as a constitutional entity has been questioned from within. Demands for home-rule came strongest from Ireland and were, of course, backed up by campaigns of violence. But demands were equally being made in Scotland for the return of Scottish institutions of governance. Indeed in Scotland as in Ireland, the union with England and Wales was never fully accepted by the population and by certain sections of the political classes and other elites. Ireland and Scotland refused to be assimilated. Relations between England and Wales were different. The term assimilation has been used to describe this relationship. However even in this relationship cultural and linguistic differences remained. Perhaps paradoxically there is a greater percentage of Welsh speakers in the "assimilated" region than there are Gaelic speakers in Scotland. This difference in historical experiences led one writer to conclude that "just as Scottish history provided opportunities for advocates of constitutional reform Welsh history trapped them, leaving the case for Welsh rights conclusively to be made".[1]

---

[1] J. Bradbury, "The Devolution Debate in Wales during the Major Governments: The Politics of a Developing Union State?" in H. Elcock and M. Keating (eds.) *Remaking the Union: Devolution and British Politics in the 1990s* (London: Frank Cass, 1998).

Background to devolution

In the early twentieth century, devolution was part of the response of the government of the day to the Irish problem. It was based on a compromise between demands for Irish independence and competing demands for the maintenance of the union.[2] For fifty years, from 1920 to 1972, the system of government in Northern Ireland was devolved.[3] The Government of Ireland Act 1920 created two Parliaments, one for the South of Ireland and one for the six counties of the North. Wide legislative powers were devolved to these two Parliaments although the ultimate aim of the scheme was to establish one system of government for the whole of Ireland. It was intended that a link between the two Parliaments would be established in the form of a Council of Ireland but this Council never met. The twin Parliament structure did not last. In 1921 an Anglo-Irish Treaty was signed and the South of Ireland became a British Dominion. The Irish Free State (Consequential Provisions) Act 1922 disapplied the 1920 Act to the southern counties of Ireland and the newly created Irish Free State laid claim to the six counties in the north. After the Second World War, the Ireland Act 1949 recognised the Republic of Ireland as an independent republic. The Irish constitution continued to lay claim to the six counties as part of the Irish nation.

The Northern Ireland Parliament, a bicameral legislature modelled on Westminster, continued to work as a devolved legislature until the system of devolution was suspended in 1972 as a result of the outbreak of sectarian violence. Throughout the period of its operation, the Northern Ireland Parliament had been dominated by the unionists, since the unionists were the majority party in Northern Ireland. The devolved Parliament was increasingly seen by the nationalist community to be oppressive and not to be protective of the interests of the Catholic community. The Northern Ireland (Temporary Provisions) Act 1972 vested extensive powers in the Secretary of State for Northern Ireland and direct rule was established. In a somewhat futile gesture towards the principle of self-

---

[2] The *Royal Commission on the Constitution 1969–73 Vol. I Report* Cmnd 5460 still remains one of the best introductions to the historical context of devolution.

[3] On earlier attempts at devolution in Northern Ireland see D. Birrell and A. Murie, *Policy and Government in Northern Ireland: Lessons of Devolution* (Dublin: Gill and MacMillan, 1980); P. Arthur, *Government and Politics of Northern Ireland* (Harlow: Longman, 1980).

determination, the Northern Ireland (Border Poll) Act 1972 provided that a referendum should be held on whether the six counties should continue to be part of the United Kingdom or be united with the Republic of Ireland. The majority of unionist voters obviously voted for the maintenance of the status quo and the majority of the nationalist community boycotted the referendum. A further attempt at devolution was made in 1973 with the Northern Ireland Assembly Act and the Northern Ireland Constitution Act but this attempt failed against a growing background of violence. The Northern Ireland Act 1974 restored direct rule.

The 1980s saw a renewed attempt to solve the problems in Northern Ireland. These attempts were the result of an increasing co-operation between the governments of the United Kingdom and the Republic of Ireland. In 1985 the Anglo-Irish Agreement, the Sunningdale Agreement, committed the United Kingdom to restore devolved government but an impasse was reached when the unionists opposed this agreement. John Major's Conservative government again tried to reach agreement with the government of the Republic of Ireland and in 1993 the Downing St Declaration signalled a major breakthrough in relations between the two governments. This Declaration was negotiated between the governments themselves but involved the political parties in Northern Ireland as part of a "Talks process". Both governments agreed that there would be no change in the status of Northern Ireland without the consent of the people of Northern Ireland and the United Kingdom agreed not to oppose any moves towards a united Ireland if consent for this course of action was shown. 1994 saw the beginnings of the period of cease-fires on the part of the IRA and the loyalist para-miltary groups and in this climate of optimism the two governments agreed in 1995 to the principles contained in the Frameworks for the Future documents.

The importance of the Frameworks documents lies not just in the institutional frameworks that were envisaged as potentially creating an accountable form of government for Northern Ireland but in the principles underlying the documents themselves. Old forms of majoritarian politics were eschewed. Instead the Frameworks documents are based on principles of "equality of opportunity, equity of treatment and parity of esteem".[4] It is explicitly stated that "there can be no going back to a system of government in Northern Ireland

---

[4] *Frameworks for the Future*, Part I Annex A para. 2.

which has the allegiance of, and is operated by, only one part of the community". Thus the 1920 model of devolution was rejected in favour of the creation of institutions involving both the communities in Northern Ireland. The new model was to be a comprehensive negotiated settlement between all parties based on a dialogue between all the political representatives and addressing "all three of the underlying relationships—those between the two parts of the community in Northern Ireland—between the two parts of Ireland and between the two Sovereign States." There was some unionist opposition to the approach taken in the Frameworks documents, particularly by some sections of the unionist community, and again an impasse was reached. John Major's very slender majority in the House of Commons meant that devolution was put on a back burner until after the general election in May 1997.

The change of government did not bring a fundamental shift in direction in relation to Northern Ireland. It did mean that a government in the United Kingdom with a very strong majority in the House of Commons and with a commitment to constitutional reform, including a commitment to devolution in Scotland and Wales, brought a strong political will to see through the process of multi-party talks begun under the Major government.

The Agreement reached in multi-party negotiations, which is also known as the Belfast Agreement or the Good Friday Agreement, was reached on April 10, 1998 and it forms the basis of the current devolution settlement for Northern Ireland.[5] In the classic style of all political compromises, the Agreement is actually an agreement to disagree. The Declaration of Support that prefaces the document accepts that what has gone before has left a "deep and profoundly regrettable legacy of suffering". The future is to be based on reconciliation, tolerance, mutual trust and a respect for human rights. The three underlying relationships recognised in the Frameworks document are to be conducted on the basis of partnership, equality and mutual respect. All parties agree to renounce violence and commit themselves to exclusively democratic and peaceful means.

---

[5] *The Agreement reached in multi-party negotiations* Cm 4292 (1998) is sometimes referred to as the Belfast Agreement or the Good Friday Agreement. It was supplemented by agreements reached between the government of the United Kingdom of Great Britain and Northern Ireland and the Government of Ireland; *Agreement Establishing Implementation Bodies* Cm 4293 (1998), *Agreement Establishing a North/South Ministerial Council* Cm 4294 (1998), *Agreement Establishing a British-Irish Intergovernmental Conference* Cm 4295 (1998), *Agreement Establishing a British-Irish Council* Cm 4296 (1998).

However, the Agreement then goes on to accept that there are deep divisions "between our continuing, and equally legitimate, political aspirations". Despite these differences however, all parties agree to try to work together in a series of inter-locking institutions. The two key institutions are the Northern Ireland Assembly and the North/South Council which are said to be so "closely inter-related that the success of each depends on that of the other".

The Agreement then commits the British and Irish governments to reach a formal Agreement on the implementation of the Belfast Agreement and this they do by annexing a formal Agreement between governments. This formal agreement sets out the commitments of both governments and creates a legally binding agreement between them which came into force after the conditions laid down in the Belfast agreement had been met in terms of constitutional reform in both countries. Both the Belfast Agreement and the Agreement between governments recognise the legitimacy of the principle of choice of the majority of the people of Northern Ireland to determine the status of Northern Ireland. This has the necessary consequence that such a choice might be exercised to remain part of the United Kingdom or to become part of a united Ireland. Both governments agree to introduce and support any necessary legislation to bring about a united Ireland should the people of Northern Ireland wish to bring this about. They also agree that the power of the government with sovereign jurisdiction in Northern Ireland will be exercised impartially and with due regard for human rights and equality principles and parity of esteem for both communities. The people of Northern Ireland may choose citizenship of either Ireland or the United Kingdom or both as their birthright and this would not change in the event of a change of status of Northern Ireland.

Under the terms of the Belfast Agreement, the United Kingdom government agreed to introduce legislation stating that Northern Ireland would remain part of the United Kingdom and would not cease to be so without the consent of the people of Northern Ireland being given in a poll. Such a poll must be held at such a time as the Secretary of State determines that the majority of people in Northern Ireland would be likely to vote in favour of a change in status of Northern Ireland. The United Kingdom government also agreed to repeal the Government of Ireland Act 1920. In its turn the Irish government agreed to amend its constitution to recognise that a united Ireland could "only be brought about by peaceful means with the consent of a majority of the people, democratically expressed, in both jurisdictions in the island".

The Agreement then sets out in three strands the institutional framework in which devolution would operate. Strand One states that there will be a democratically elected Assembly in Northern Ireland exercising legislative and executive functions but subject to a number of safeguards to protect the rights and interests of all sides of the community. Strand Two provides for an all-Ireland Council, the North/South Ministerial Council, to develop "consultation, co-operation and action" within the island of Ireland. Strand Three creates the British-Irish Council to "promote harmonious and mutually beneficial development of the totality of relationships" amongst the peoples of "these islands" to include representation from all the devolved administrations.

The remaining parts of the Belfast Agreement set out other related issues and put the institutional framework into a context whereby the concerns of both sides of the community can begin to be addressed. The human rights agenda of the nationalists, for example, resulted in the creation of a Northern Ireland Human Rights Commission whereas the concerns of the unionists over decommissioning of weapons were met by a commitment on all sides to participate in the Independent Commission on decommissioning. Other issues included policing, security, review of the criminal justice system and prisoners. All of these issues are central to the Agreement and are mutually inter-dependent.

The two governments agreed to hold separate referenda on May 22, 1998 and subject to approval being given in each referendum would then prepare legislation. On the part of the United Kingdom this would mean legislation to establish a New Northern Ireland Assembly in shadow-mode followed by legislation to establish the Northern Ireland Assembly and to transfer powers to it. That legislation would also deal with other related matters such as the creation of the Human Right Commission. Separate legislation would deal with prisoner releases and policing issues. In the referendum in Northern Ireland, 71.2 per cent of those voting voted in favour of the Belfast Agreement. In the Republic of Ireland 94 per cent of those voting voted in favour of the constitutional amendments required.

The Northern Ireland (Elections) Act 1998 created the New Northern Ireland Assembly whose purpose was to take "part in part in preparations to give effect to the agreement reached in multi-party negotiations".[6] Members of the 108 strong New Northern Ireland

---

[6] Northern Ireland (Elections) Act 1998, s.1.

Assembly were elected in June 1998.[7] The Northern Ireland Act 1998 translates into legislative form the terms of the Belfast Agreement in relation to principles of consent, the transfer of legislative and executive powers to the Northern Ireland Assembly and the establishment of the Northern Ireland Human Rights Commission. It also creates an Equality Commission for Northern Ireland. It is this piece of legislation that is the focus of this book. The Northern Ireland Act 1998 provided that the Secretary of State would by Order determine the appointed day for the transfer of powers if it appears "that sufficient progress has been made in implementing the Belfast Agreement". Despite lengthy delays, particularly over issues of decommissioning of weapons, the Secretary of State did lay such an Order and the Northern Ireland Assembly came into existence in December 1999 thereby replacing the New Northern Ireland Assembly.[8] No sooner had devolution occurred than the Secretary of State determined that insurmountable political disagreements over decommissioning were a threat to the operation of devolved government and fresh legislation was enacted to suspend the operation of devolved government in Northern Ireland. Under powers granted by the Northern Ireland Act 2000 the Secretary of State suspended devolution and the entire process went into review. That review terminated in May 2000 when Peter Mandelson as Secretary of State restored devolution, again under powers granted by the Northern Ireland Act 2000.[9] Thus devolved government was restored in Northern Ireland on May 30, 2000.

By contrast, devolution to Scotland has been comparatively straightforward. The experiment in legislative devolution to Northern Ireland in the earlier part of the twentieth century has no parallel in Scotland. Instead a form of executive devolution took place with the expansion of the role of Secretary of State for Scotland and the creation of the Scottish Office. It has been said that the main period of expansion of the Scottish Office was between 1920–1940[10] and that support for the "managerial control of the implementation of policy" that this expansion brought was supported by the major

---

[7] The results of the election, the franchise and the structure of the New Northern Ireland Assembly are discussed in the following chapter.

[8] S.I. 1999/3208 The Northern Ireland Act 1998 (Appointed Day) Order 1999.

[9] S.I. 2000/1445 The Northern Ireland Act 2000 (Restoration of Devolved Government) Order 2000.

[10] A. Brown, D. McCrone and L. Paterson, *Politics and Society in Scotland* (Basingstoke: Mamillan Press, 1998) at 13.

political parties in Scotland. Thus the Labour Party abandoned its earlier campaigns for a Scottish Parliament of the kind that had been established in Northern Ireland.[11] Only the Scottish Nationalist Party, founded in the 1930s, agitated for a Scottish Parliament.

In 1969, when the Royal Commission on the Constitution was appointed "there was obviously some discontent with the workings of government, and the outward signs of that discontent seemed to reflect especially the frustrations of those living furthest from London.[12]" Economic problems were at the root of this discontent with the perception that United Kingdom policies were insufficient to meet the problems of large-scale industrial decline. The Royal Commission recommended that legislative and executive powers should be devolved to a Scottish Parliament. The Labour Government enacted the Scotland Act 1978, which would have created a Scottish Parliament. The Act was repealed following a referendum in Scotland when only 32.5 per cent of the electorate voted in favour of devolution. The referendum required a 40 per cent vote.

The campaign for a Scottish Parliament continued and in 1988 a Scottish Constitutional Convention was established "to make plans for the future governance of Scotland[13]." Members of the Scottish Constitutional Convention were self-appointed but membership was drawn from a wide range of Scottish organisations, political parties, trade unions, local authorities and voluntary group and agencies. The final report of the Convention was published in 1995 as *Scotland's Parliament: Scotland's Right*. As its name suggests, this report advocated the creation of a Scottish Parliament and the transfer of legislative powers over a wide range of matters. Throughout the life of the Convention, the government in London was Conservative. The Conservative Party had no interest in devolved government and it was not until a change of government in May 1997 that the aspirations of the Scottish Constitutional Convention could be met.

Two months after the election, the Labour government set out its plans for a Scottish Parliament in its White Paper.[14] The proposals for

---

[11] A. Brown *et al.* in note 10, 15.

[12] *Royal Commission on the Constitution 1969–73 Vol I*, 3.

[13] Discussed in L. Paterson, *A Diverse Assembly: The Debate on a Scottish Parliament* (Edinburgh: EUP, 1998), N. Burrows, "Unfinished Business: The Scotland Act 1998" (1999) 62 *Modern Law Review* 241, R. McLean, "A Brief History of Scottish Home Rule" in G. Hassan (ed) *A Guide to the Scottish Parliament* (Edinburgh: The Stationery Office, 1999).

[14] *Scotland's Parliament* Cm 3658 (1997).

legislation outlined in the White Paper were put to a referendum in September 1997. The referendum indicated widespread popular support for the creation of a Parliament and for that Parliament to have tax varying powers. On a turnout of 60.4 per cent, 74.3 per cent voted in favour of the creation of a Scottish parliament with 25.7 per cent against. 65.5 per cent voted in favour of tax varying powers with 36.5 per cent against. In light of this success, the Scotland Bill was published in December 1997 and the Scotland Act subsequently received Royal Assent in November 1998. The first elections took place in May 1999.

Following the outcome of the successful referendum, the Minister responsible for devolution in Scotland, Henry McLeish, appointed a group of individuals to work as a Consultative Steering Group on the Scottish Parliament (CSG). The function of this group was to "bring together views on and consider the operational needs and working methods of the Scottish Parliament".[15] The CSG consulted widely on the operation of the new Parliament and produced its final report in December 1998. This report provided the basis for the initial standing orders of the new Scottish Parliament including recommendations on the role of its committees and on the key principles that its members believed should be adopted by the Parliament in its work.

In Wales, devolution has taken a very different path.[16] Executive devolution to Wales of the kind seen in Scotland from the 1920s onwards was developed in Wales after the Second World War. The creation of the Welsh Office and the Cabinet post of Secretary of State for Wales was a way of giving a distinctive Welsh voice in the government of the United Kingdom. However, there did not appear to be a strong feeling towards devolution in Wales, largely because the Labour Party, the largest political party in Wales, itself was divided on the issue. The attempt to create an elected Assembly by the enactment of the Wales Act 1978 failed due to lack of popular support just as the attempt to create a Scottish Parliament had in that year. The Wales Act would have created an Assembly with executive but no legislative powers.

In the 1980s and early 1990s Welsh politics became increasingly divorced from the Thatcherite policies being pursued by central

---

[15] *Shaping Scotland's Parliament* (Edinburgh: The Scottish Office, 1998).
[16] J. Bradbury, in note 1 above, 120.

government. Margaret Thatcher appeared to have no understanding of Welsh sensibilities appointing four Secretaries of State for Wales from M.Ps from English constituencies. During this period the Labour Party in Wales moved towards an acceptance of the need for devolution. Ron Davies suggests that "the re-emergence of devolution back onto the Labour Party's agenda was fuelled by the impact of successive election losses and facilitated by pressure for local government reform".[17] The Poll Tax created resentment across the United Kingdom and in Wales debates about reform of local government became linked to the need for an elected Assembly to co-ordinate policy. Between 1987–1989 the Labour Party in Wales accepted the need to establish an Assembly as part of an overall package of regional reform. When Ron Davies was appointed as Shadow Secretary of State for Wales in 1992, he argued that "modern socialism must empower people and . . . devolution is central to this vision . . . it represents a key part of the modern Labour Party's philosophy".[18] In May 1995 the Welsh Labour Party discussed proposals for devolution, *Shaping the Vision*, at its conference in Llandudno and from then on devolution to Wales became one of the key ideas in New Labour's plans for constitutional reform.

After the election in May 1997, the new government published its White Paper, *Voice for Wales* in which it was proposed to establish an elected Assembly with executive but not legislative powers.[19] As in Scotland, these proposals were put to a referendum but in Wales the result was much closer. On a turnout of 51 per cent, 50.3 per cent voted in favour of the proposition "I agree that there should be a Welsh Assembly" whilst 49.7 per cent voted for the contrary proposition. The vote was won with an overall majority of 6721 votes. The Welsh electorate was therefore almost equally divided on the question of devolution. Notwithstanding the narrow support base for devolution, the government introduced the Government of Wales Bill which received Royal Assent in July 1998. The first elections were held in May 1999 and functions were transferred to the National Assembly for Wales on July 1, 1999.[20]

The Welsh equivalent of the Scottish CSG was the National Assembly Advisory Group (NAAG). NAAG was set up by the

---

[17] R. Davies, *Devolution: A Process not an Event* (Cardiff: Institute for Welsh Affairs, 1999) at 4.
[18] R. Davies in note 17, at 6.
[19] *Voice for Wales* Cm 3718 (1997).
[20] S.I. 1999/672 *The National Assembly for Wales (Transfer of Functions) Order 1999.*

Secretary of State for Wales in December 1997. It was to assist the Secretary of State in preparation of guidance for standing orders and to advise the Secretary of State on the operation of the National Assembly. NAAG consulted widely on these matters and produced its final report in August 1998.[21]

New Labour and constitutional reform

The key theme underlying New Labour's programme of constitutional reform is "modernisation". Tony Blair has said that his "Government has a mission to modernise".[22] However, what is not made explicit is what a modern constitution for the United Kingdom might look like.[23] Devolution to Scotland, Northern Ireland and Wales is part of the constitutional reform agenda but so too is reform of the House of Lords, the introduction of human rights and freedom of information legislation and the creation of an Assembly and mayor for London. Most of these proposals for reform had been circulating well before the Labour Party re-invented itself as New Labour. Nor is it clear what constitutional models might be used to guide the United Kingdom towards its modern goal. Modern does not appear to be used in the sense of "recent". New Labour has not looked elsewhere to countries with newly adopted constitutions and borrowed directly from them. Any numbers of recent constitutions abound in Eastern Europe. Spain adopted her most recent constitution in 1978. This constitution was based on the recognition of demands for regional self-government and might have provided a useful template for a modern constitution for the United Kingdom.

In the context of Scottish devolution, although the point is equally valid in Northern Ireland, Nairn has argued that the rejection of a more deep-rooted reform by New Labour has resulted in the birth of a "kind of constitution-less semi-statehood".[24] Nairn argues that

---

[21] *National Assembly for Wales: have your say on how it will work* (Cardiff: The Welsh Office, 1998). *National Assembly Advisory Group Report to the Secretary of State for Wales* (Cardiff, the Welsh Office, 1998).

[22] *Modernising Government* Cm 4310 (1999).

[23] For a discussion of the government's legislative programme in relation to constitutional reform see R. Hazell, "Reinventing the Constitution: Can the State Survive?" (1999) *Public Law* at 84.

[24] T. Nairn, "A New Song for Scotland: The Making of the Scottish Constitution" in G. Hassan and C. Warhurst (eds) *A Different Future: A Moderniser's Guide to Scotland* (Glasgow: The Big Issue in Scotland, 1999) at 49.

limiting the reform of the constitution to "those bits of archaic statehood . . . devolution, control of interest rates, the arrangements in Northern Ireland or the House of Lords" means that New Labour's programme is based on a belief that "the revised old order might work better than ever". In other words, that devolution and other constitutional reforms are merely intended to reinforce the existing order within the United Kingdom and do not have a radical or socialist edge. This approach sees devolution as a denial of identity politics and a means of bolstering the United Kingdom. As such, Nairn argues, devolution is doomed to failure since it renders the ancient order "irretrievably unstable" and does not provide a framework for lasting change.

Morison too challenges the view that the Blairite reform agenda is in fact modern.[25] Despite describing Tony Blair as "the most far-reaching, radical reformer of the formal edifice of the constitution since Oliver Cromwell" Morison argues that the "problem with the Labour government proposals is that they are wrongly focused on the traditional agenda of restraining 'big government' and shoring up ideas of representative government". The constitutional reform project, he argues, is aimed at the wrong target. What is missing is "a radical agenda of constitutional renewal" that "will acknowledge the complexity and the fugitive nature of power and seek to exercise democratic control in the new sites where power is exercised". Morison's solution is to "move beyond the limits of traditional liberal individualist democracy towards the establishment of an idea of a constitution as a preference-forming network".

By contrast, Ron Davies is less dogmatic and, at the same time, more optimistic about New Labour's conversion to devolution. He outlines the arguments within the Welsh Labour Party about devolution, showing how it moved from outright opposition to accommodation with identity politics.[26] Devolution, he argues, is part of the process of making politics in Wales "less tribal and dogmatic". His view of devolution, and his view carried the day, was that the state centred approach of Labour excluded and alienated people from the democratic process. To him, devolution was a means of widening democracy. It was Davies, for example, who persuaded Tony Blair to

---

[25] J. Morison, "The Case Against Constitutional Reform", (1998) at 25 *Journal of Law and Society* at 510.
[26] R. Davies, *Devolution: A Process not an Event* (Cardiff: Institute for Welsh Affairs, 1999).

include the term "inclusiveness" in his speech to the Welsh Labour Party in 1996. There was a feeling both in Wales and Scotland that politics were not representative. Policies decided in Westminster did not reflect the wishes of the electorates in these areas. In particular, the excesses of Thatcherism had been rejected in successive elections. Labour had to restore a belief in politics itself and could do this by widening participation and listening to alternative views.

In the Government's White Paper on modernisation, Tony Blair tells us clearly what he considers to be "outdated". "Old arguments are now out-dated—big government against small government, interventionism against laissez-faire". "The right issues", he tells us are "modernising government, better government, getting government right".[27] Modern government is better government and better government is modern. This somewhat circular argument is repeated by Jack Cunningham in the same White Paper. According to him, a modern government is one that delivers services better and one that needs, therefore "joined-up government . . . integrated government . . . the best and most modern techniques". Underlying this approach are the twin keystones of the strategy: inclusiveness and integration. In short, modern government is government that delivers services to the citizen in the most efficient way—hence joined-up or integrated government. Government must be responsive by allowing citizens into the policy-making process about the kind of services they require—hence inclusiveness.

It would seem that the need for integrated and efficient central government would run against the dispersal of responsibility for government within the United Kingdom. Devolution would seem to be neither integrated nor joined-up government. Responsibility for policy making and implementation is dispersed on a geographical basis thus creating at least the possibility that policy divergences will exist in the different parts of the United Kingdom. Levels of performance might equally diverge. The solution to these potential problems lies in other key elements of New Labour strategies. Integrated and efficient services can be delivered through partnership and co-operation.

However, it is clear that New Labour equates modernisation, or at least one aspect of modernisation, with devolution of power to what might be termed the non-English regions of the United Kingdom.

---

[27] *Modernising Government* Cm 4310 (1999).

Devolution does not restore these regions to the status quo ante, *i.e.* to their position before the various Acts of Union incorporated them into the United Kingdom. The United Kingdom, in this modern version, remains as a nation state, strengthened and renewed by devolution, looking forward and not back. "Self-government for the nations and regions of the United Kingdom is seen not as a nostalgic remnant of the past but as a central element in political, social and economic modernisation".[28]

It is possible to analyse New Labour's views on the relationship between devolution and modernisation by an analysis of the white papers published in the summer of 1997.[29] In terms of constitutional reform and devolution, "modernisation" can be analysed in terms of objectives, methods and principles. In taking this approach it is possible to challenge some of the criticisms laid at the constitutional reform project by Morison. It is clear that the creation of institutions is part of a wider strategy of renewal. The objectives underlying the devolution project go beyond the mere creation of institutions towards creating a new framework of government that is as much a facilitator of locally developed projects as a provider of solutions to locally perceived needs.

Objectives

There appear to be at least 10 objectives underlying the devolution programme. They can be summarised as follows:

- to clean up politics
- to increase individual rights
- to address problems of the democratic deficit
- to provide control over public spending
- to ensure high standards of public service
- to provide for accountability
- to encourage sustainable economic development

---

[28] M. Keating and H. Elcock, "Devolution and the UK State" in H. Elcock and M. Keating in note 1, 3.
[29] *Scotland's Parliament* Cm 3658 (1997); *National Assembly for Wales* Cm 3719 (1997).

- to move the process of decision making closer to the citizen

- to complete the chain of democratic accountability (from local to E.U.)

- to reduce the role of QUANGOs and transfer their functions to elected authorities.

These objectives can be grouped together under broader headings: strengthening the democratic process, restoration of public confidence in political institutions, protecting the citizen against the abuses of power and assisting in economic development. In Northern Ireland, where devolution is part of a much wider constitutional settlement, two additional of objectives can be noted:

- to secure a peaceful settlement of the troubles

- to normalise relations with the Republic of Ireland.

These are very broad objectives. Devolution is seen as a way of rejuvenating the non-English parts of the United Kingdom politically and economically. In political terms, the former Scottish, Welsh and Northern Ireland Offices are brought under the control of regional elected bodies. In economic terms, the regions become the focus for economic regeneration.

There may be a gulf between the stated objectives and the underlying objectives of policy. Devolution, for example, may be a ploy to "ditch the nats" and to silence the real opposition to the Labour Party in Scotland or Wales. The method of election to the Scottish Parliament and the National Assembly for Wales, in effect, silences nationalist demands. The division of seats into constituency and regional seats plus the method of election virtually guarantees that there will never be an overwhelming majority of any party in the Scottish Parliament or the National Assembly for Wales. In particular it is unlikely that the Scottish National Party (SNP) or Plaid Cymru will ever muster sufficient strength to use the Parliament as a stepping stone to independence. Devolution, therefore, is intended to secure the union in Great Britain. Political inclusiveness therefore means inclusiveness within the existing constitutional order of the British union state.

Methods

Five methods have been chosen to attain these objectives:

- decentralisation of power
- creation of new institutions
- opening up of government
- reform of parliament
- rationalisation of existing structures (for Wales)

These methods, in particular the issues of decentralisation and institution building are the focus of this book. All the planned institutions have now been established. In the early stages, the emphasis has been on agenda setting and prioritisation as well as on the methods of co-ordination of policy amongst the devolved institutions.

Principles

The fundamental principle underlying the entire process of devolution is one of consent. Before the adoption of the devolution legislation, the consent of the people in the region was obtained in a referendum. However, the principle of consent has two meanings. In Wales and Scotland the people in those regions were asked whether they supported the creation of an Assembly (Wales) or Parliament (Scotland). Consent in this context means consent to the creation of new institutions within the framework of the United Kingdom. New Labour rejected the demands of the SNP for a referendum on Scottish independence. Consent was evidenced in both cases by a simple majority of those voting in the referenda.

This type of consent was called "popular consent" by Donald Dewar during the debate on the Referendums (Scotland and Wales) Bill. He argued that popular consent provided moral legitimacy and moral authority for the government's scheme of devolution.

In the case of Northern Ireland an entire package of measures was placed before the peoples of Ireland, north and south. Part of that package was an agreement on the part of the government of Ireland to reform its own constitution laying claim to the north of Ireland

and at the same time an agreement on the part of the United Kingdom to provide in legislation for the principle of consent. Popular consent was obtained in Northern Ireland for the package of measures. In the referendum 71.2 per cent of those voting voted in favour of the Belfast Agreement. In the Republic of Ireland a referendum was legally required to amend the constitution. That support was amply demonstrated with a 94 per cent vote in favour of the constitutional amendment.

However in Northern Ireland consent needs to be on-going. Consent in this context means consent to remain part of the United Kingdom. The Northern Ireland Act provides that Northern Ireland will form part of the territory of the United Kingdom until a wish is "expressed by a majority" that this status be changed and Northern Ireland become part of a united Ireland.[30] Consent is not merely to the establishment of institutions of government in Northern Ireland but consent to accept British sovereignty and retain a British identity. There is no equivalent principle found in the other two devolution settlements. Under these settlements, the Scots and the Welsh remain indefinitely British.

Principles applying to the devolved administrations

The new institutions are to be based on principles of[31]:

- inclusiveness
- diversity
- sustainability
- equal opportunity
- modern working practices
- flexibility and responsiveness
- openness and accessibility

---

[30] For a discussion of the variety of interpretations that have been developed in respect of these provisions see B. Hadfield, "The Belfast Agreement, Sovereignty and the State of the Union" [1998] P.L. Winter at 599.
[31] *Shaping Scotland's Parliament* in note . . . and *National Assembly Advisory Group Report to the Secretary of State for Wales* in note 20.

It is, of course difficult to legislate for principles such as these. They are merely words unless and until translated into reality. However, it is interesting that principles such as inclusiveness and equal opportunity have been chosen as part of the language of devolution. It is certainly the case that a considerable effort has been made at least to try to live up to many of these principles in these early days. Access to information on the work of the various committees of the devolved institutions, for example, is made easier by the publication of papers and materials on the various web sites. Extensive consultations have taken place on aspects of policy and on agenda setting issues. Equal opportunities committees have been established in Wales and Scotland. In elections to the parliamentary bodies in these regions there was a determined attempt to get more women into politics so that in Wales 42 per cent of AMs are female and in Scotland 37 per cent of MSPs. However, to its shame, there are no ethnic minority representatives in the Scottish Parliament and women have only five of the 22 Ministerial appointments.

The emphasis to date has been on institution building and institutional reform. The underlying assumption is that if institutions perform effectively and efficiently then politics will be cleaned up, democracy strengthened and the other objectives of the modernisation programme will be achieved. The emphasis in the legislation is therefore on the creation of institutions to which functions and competencies are transferred. Some functions are common. The Welsh Assembly, the Northern Ireland Assembly and the Scottish Parliament are all involved in policy formulation. They each have a role in the control of spending and in holding regional "governments" or executives to account. However the range of competencies differs significantly. The Welsh Assembly does not have the power to adopt primary legislation unlike the Northern Ireland or Scottish institutions. The Scottish Parliament has a tax varying power.

Thus New Labour's scheme of devolution is asymmetrical. Lack of symmetry is not, in itself, a problem. As Keating demonstrates, asymmetrical constitutional settlements "abound".[32] Keating defends the asymmetrical approach in the context of the United Kingdom by arguing that the United Kingdom is a union state. He defines a union state as "a state without a formal federal division of powers but in

---

[32] M. Keating, "What's Wrong with Asymmetrical Government?" in H. Elcock and M. Keating in note 1, at 202.

which parts of the territory have been incorporated by treaty and agreement". The union state is "often asymmetrical in origin". Certainly this is the case in the United Kingdom. For example, the Acts of Union between Scotland and England preserved the integrity of key Scottish institutions whereas the earlier union with Wales is defined in terms of assimilation. The existence of a separate legal order in Scotland, for example, distinguishes the Welsh and Scottish positions.

There is a danger, however, of failing to distinguish asymmetrical devolution from haphazard devolution. Underlying the current devolution process, there is no clear constitutional model. Each devolution settlement has been a response to local demands and needs and there has been no attempt to provide a legal framework within which the regional governments will operate. This is a pragmatic rather than a principled approach. Our modern constitution is therefore unstructured and flexible.

New Labour's approach to devolution in the United Kingdom is at best asymmetrical and at worst haphazard. It is certainly complex. What appears to be lacking at present is the recognition of the need for constitutional principles within which the various devolution settlements can operate. It is here that New Labour's modernisation process is weakest. There is an absence of constitutional rules and principles to be applied to the United Kingdom's constitutional structure as a whole. The development of these principles is being left to convention and political agreements.[33] Given political will, this can be a successful way to manage multi-layered democracy. In the absence of political will and of constitutional guarantees or principles, New Labour's model of devolution might prove, in the long run, to be irredeemably unstable.

---

[33] Discussed in Chapter 5 below.

Chapter 2

Parliamentary institutions

It is the intention of the New Labour government that the principles examined in Chapter 1 will underpin the new devolved institutions. The primary legislation goes some way to provide a framework in which these principles can be guaranteed but the legislation is precisely that, a framework. It is in the day to day running of the devolved administrations where principles of openness, inclusiveness, equality and so on will be important. Principles can, to some extent, be built into structures and procedures and there has been an attempt to do so in the institutional structures and rules of procedure of the devolved parliamentary bodies. The day to day operations of the parliamentary bodies are governed by standing orders. The initial standing orders of all three institutions were adopted by Order of the Westminster Parliament and are a deliberate attempt to give a steer to the new institutions in the direction of modernisation.

This chapter compares the Scottish Parliament, the National Assembly for Wales and the Northern Ireland Assembly in terms of composition and structure. The purpose of the comparison is to explore the differences between the institutions in structural terms. The functions of the three elected bodies are discussed in the following chapter. In terms of types of membership and methods of election there are similarities between the Scottish Parliament and the National Assembly for Wales but they both differ from the Northern Ireland Assembly in both these respects. In all three institutions there has been an emphasis on committee structures but the function and purposes of the committees differ. The chapter attempts to account for these differences and similarities.

This chapter uses the term "parliamentary" to describe the Scottish Parliament, the National Assembly for Wales and the

Northern Ireland Assembly. The term may be misleading if it is understood in the sense of being the legislature. The National Assembly for Wales is not a parliament in the sense of being a legislative assembly. Devolution to Wales is executive devolution.[1] The National Assembly for Wales is a body corporate based on a modified cabinet style of government.[2] Primary legislation for Wales will continue to be adopted in Westminster. These functional differences are explored in the following chapter. "Parliamentary" is used in this chapter therefore to denote the elected bodies, the Scottish Parliament, the Northern Ireland Assembly and the National Assembly for Wales.

Franchise

The franchise for elections to the Scottish Parliament, the Welsh Assembly and the Northern Ireland Assembly is expressed in terms of eligibility to vote in local rather than Westminster elections.[3] This definition gives the right to vote, therefore, to persons entitled to vote for elections to the House of Commons and also to E.U. nationals and to peers. It is possible to explain this approach in one of two ways. Either the devolved administrations are being compared to rather grand local authorities or an attempt is being made to widen the franchise in line with principles of openness and inclusiveness.

Members and constituencies

The Scotland Act and the Government of Wales Act provide for two types of members; constituency and regional members.[4] In Scotland one constituency Member of the Scottish Parliament (MSP) is to be elected per constituency. These are the 72 Westminster constituencies although Orkney and Shetland are treated as

---

[1] This point becomes clearer in the discussion of the functions of the National Assembly for Wales in Chapter 3 below.
[2] For an excellent discussion of the Welsh arrangements see R. Rawlings, "The New Model Wales" (1998) at 25 *Journal of Law and Society* 461.
[3] The Scotland Act s.11; the Government of Wales Act s.10; the Northern Ireland (Elections) Act s.2.
[4] Scotland Act, s.5.

two constituencies. For the purposes of the first elections for the Scottish Parliament, therefore, there were 73 constituencies.[5] The 73 constituency MSPs are elected on the basis of a simple majority vote (first past the post). In addition, there are 56 MSPs elected by an additional member system from "regions" of Scotland. The closed list system is used in the elections for the Scottish Parliament. This means that political parties list their candidates in the order in which they are selected and voters cannot express any preference for one candidate over another on the list. The regions are defined in terms of the old European constituencies as defined in the European Parliamentary Constituencies (Scotland) Order 1996. There are therefore eight such regional constituencies each returning seven regional MSPs. This makes a total of 129 MSPs with constituency MSPs being in the majority. The effect of tying Westminster and Scottish constituencies will become apparent within the next decade when the number of Scottish seats in Westminster is due to be reduced by some 15–20 seats. If the linkage between Westminster and Holyrood constituencies is maintained, the Scottish Parliament will also be reduced in size.

The basis of election of Assembly Members in Wales is the same. 40 constituency AMs are elected by simple majority vote (first past the post) with constituencies for the Assembly being the same as those for Westminster elections.[6] In addition, 20 regional AMs are elected from the five European constituencies specified in the European Parliamentary Constituencies (Wales) Order 1994. This makes a total of 60 AMs. There are no plans to reduce the size of the National Assembly for Wales and Schedule 1 of the Government of Wales Act requires the Boundary Commission for Wales to take into consideration the effect of any recommendation on the composition of the Assembly.

Constituency and regional members are intended to be equal in every respect. The issue of equality was raised in one of the early debates of the Scottish Parliament. The point in issue was the level of allowances to be paid to MSPs. It had been mooted during the passage of the Scotland Bill that MSPs might be paid at different levels but this idea had been rejected. All MSPs receive the same basic pay and pensions.[7] They do not however receive the same

---

[5] Scotland Act, Sched 1.
[6] Government of Wales Act, s.2.
[7] The Scotland Act 1998, s.81. See S.I. 1999/1081, S.I. 1999/1082 and S.I. 1999/1097 for rules on payments and pensions.

level of allowances. The Parliament established a Members' Allowances Scheme to be administered and supervised by the Scottish Parliamentary Corporate Body (SPCB).[8] The Scheme provides that all Members are to be treated equally in respect of their travel, accommodation and staffing allowances. However, constituency MSPs are each provided with an allowance to cover the costs of running a constituency office. Regional MSPs receive only one third of this allowance and the regional MSPs belonging to a particular political party are expected to pool these costs to establish an office within their region. MSPs from the larger regions may establish two regional offices with the consent of the SPCB and additional allowances are paid accordingly. This question did not arise in the National Assembly for Wales since both types of AMs are paid the same level of allowances.

The debates on the level of allowances may appear to be banal if not grasping but they do underlie the serious point as to the functions to be accorded to different types of members. Who, for example, should deal with a particular matter raised by a constituent? To whom should a constituent turn with a problem? Will "turf wars" develop between constituency and regional MSPs and between MSPs and MPs? Some of these issues are addressed in a statement of principles that forms part of the Allowances Scheme. They can be summarised as follows:

- any constituent can approach any of his/her eight MSPs
- if a constituent wants to approach a particular MSP, he/she must be directed to that MSP by all others
- all MSPs have the right to hold surgeries within the region for which they were returned
- a constituent who approaches an MSP with a constituency issue should be directed to a relevant MSP, *i.e* any of the eight MSPs within the region and not just the constituency MSP
- a list MSP who raises a constituency issue should notify the constituency MSP unless the consent of the constituent is withheld
- MSPs approached by constituents on any reserved matter (*e.g.* social security) should refer the constituent to their MP.

---

[8] Scottish Parliament Official Record (SPOR) 1999, Vol. 1, No. 7, Cols 333–344.

It is difficult to predict how far these principles will be upheld. It is certainly the case that many Westminster MPs deal with issues relating to the work of local authorities—it would politically naïve to believe that any MSP approached by a voter or a potential voter would refer the matter to another MSP particularly one from a different party. During the debates over allowances it was clear that the Labour Party did not anticipate that regional MSPs would have the same level of contact with constituents and hence there was little need for regional MSPs to have an office allowance. Given that the bulk of regional MSPs are not Labour, this is not surprising. SNP Members rejected this view absolutely and demanded the same level of support arguing that constituents now had a choice of which MSP to approach. In the end a Liberal Democrat compromise was accepted as outlined above.

There are 108 members of the New Northern Ireland Assembly. Six members are elected from the eighteen Westminster constituencies.[9] In Northern Ireland therefore the distinction between constituency and list members does not arise.

The size of each of the parliamentary institutions is not based on population. The difference in approach to the number of members and constituencies is explicable in terms of the background of each institution. The arrangements for the Scottish Parliament were first proposed by the Scottish Constitutional Convention.[10] Haggerty reports that the figure of 129 was chosen as a compromise between the Liberal Democrats who had wanted an almost 50:50 split between constituency and regional members to ensure a balance between members elected on the basis of proportional representation and members elected on a first past the post system. This would have resulted in a Parliament of 145 members. As against this, the Labour Party, wanting a greater emphasis on first past the post, argued for a Parliament of 112 of which 40 would be regional members. 129 was a compromise between these two positions.[11] It was a compromise that was accepted by the Labour Party and continued through into the legislation. The Northern Ireland

---

[9] Northern Ireland (Elections) Act, s.1.
[10] Discussed in Chapter 1 above.
[11] C. Haggerty, "Electing the Scottish Parliament: Smoke-filled rooms or Greater Democracy?" in T. St J. N. Bates (ed) *Devolution to Scotland: the Legal Aspects* (Edinburgh: T & T Clark, 1997).

Assembly of 108 members is larger than its predecessors.[12] The figure of 108 was arrived at during the negotiations of the Belfast Agreement and is intended to ensure a greater degree of inclusiveness in representation.[13] The National Assembly for Wales has 60 members. This is smaller than had been proposed under the Wales Act 1978 which had envisaged an Assembly of 80 members. Rawlings explains the reduction in size in terms of intervention by the central Labour Party which required the Labour Party in Wales to consider an element of proportionality into the system of election along the lines proposed for Scotland.[14] The element of proportionality in Wales is much less than in Scotland, a fact Rawlings attributes to a Labour Party desire to retain control. The White Paper explains the degree of proportionality in terms of a system that will ensure "that the Assembly reflects the diversity of modern Wales geographically, culturally and politically".[15] Thus it is not only the size of the parliamentary institutions that differs but the degree of proportional representation built into the system. The Northern Ireland Assembly is elected entirely on the basis of proportional representation. The Scottish Parliament is 73:56 and the National Assembly for Wales is 60:40.

Methods of election

The Scotland Act and the Government of Wales Act provide that each elector has two votes. The first vote is cast for the constituency member and the second is for a registered political party that has submitted a list, or for an individual candidate. In both cases it is only after the constituency members have been elected that the regional votes come into play.[16] To determine the allocation of regional seats the total number of votes cast for a party is divided between the number of seats gained in the constituency poll plus one and this process is repeated until all the regional seats are filled.

---

[12] Under the Government of Ireland Act 1920, there were 52 elected members of the House of Commons and under the 1973 Northern Ireland Assembly Act there was to have been an elected chamber of 78 members.
[13] *Agreement reached in multi-party negotiations* Cm 4292 (1998), Strand One.
[14] R. Rawlings in note 2 475.
[15] *A Voice for Wales* Cm 3718 (1998).
[16] Scotland Act, s.7, Government of Wales Act, s.4.

The political parties list their candidates (up to a maximum of 12) and regional seats are allocated to candidates in the order of party preference.[17]

This system is a compromise between the Liberal Democratic desire for proportional representation and the Labour attachment to first past the post. It introduces an element of proportionality into the elected institutions. It is said to be part of the process of developing inclusive and modern politics into the United Kingdom system of governance but it also has the effect of reducing the overall impact of the nationalist vote. The results of the first elections in Scotland and Wales produced no overall majority and in Scotland this has led to a coalition between the Party gaining the most seats, Labour, and the fourth largest party, the Liberal Democrats. In Wales, Labour was the largest party but did not have an overall majority and Labour opted to become a minority administration.

The results of the elections were a disappointment to Labour but they could be cloaked in terms of the "new politics". The new system of election was intended to spread seats on a more proportional basis and it was clear that the Labour Party would lose its stranglehold on politics in both regions. The system was intended to encourage a new consensual type of politics with an element of power sharing. The New Labour government could not have foreseen just how much power would have to be shared.

The first elections for the Scottish Parliament were held on May 6, 1999. The turnout for the elections at about 59 per cent was much lower than had been the case for the referendum on the creation of the Parliament. As can be seen from the tables below, no party won an overall majority in the new Parliament. The additional member system guaranteed seats to those parties who had not won a significant number of constituency seats. The Scottish Conservative Party, for example, with no constituency seats gained 18 list members. It also allowed two seats to be won by small political parties. Tommy Sheridan was elected in the Glasgow region for Scotland's newest political party, the Scottish Socialist Party. Robin Harper was elected in the Lothians for the Green Party, giving that party its first electoral victory in a parliamentary election.

---

[17] Scotland Act, s.8, Government of Wales Act, s.6.

Overall results

Party	No. of seats
Labour	56
SNP	35
Lib Dems	17
Conservatives	18
Greens	1
SSP	1
Independent	1
Total	129

Constituency seats

Party	No. of seats	per cent of vote
Labour	53	39%
SNP	7	29%
Lib Dems	12	14%
Conservatives	0	16%
Independent Canavan★	1	N/A
Total	73	

★ Denis Canavan is the only MSP in the first Parliament not to belong to any political party.

Regional seats

Party	No. of seats	% of vote
Labour	3	35%
SNP	28	29%
Lib Dems	5	13%
Conservatives	18	16%
Greens	1	4%
SSP	1	2%
Total	56	2%

The first elections to the National Assembly for Wales also took place on May 6, 1999. The turnout in Wales was significantly lower than in Scotland, averaging at 40 per cent. This is line with the turnout for the referendum. As was the case with Scotland, Labour won a majority of the constituency seats but failed to win an overall majority in the Assembly.

Overall results

Party	No. of seats
Labour	28
PC	17
Lib Dems	6
Conservatives	9
Total	60

Constituency seats

Party	No. of seats	% of vote
Labour	27	36%
PC	9	33%
Lib Dems	3	13%
Conservatives	1	15%
Total	40	

Regional seats

Party	No. of seats	% of vote
Labour	1	36%
PC	8	30%
Lib Dems	3	12%
Conservatives	8	16%
Total	20	

These results show the effect of the new voting system. The Labour Party gained 53 of the 73 constituency seats in Scotland and 27 of the 40 in Wales with 39 per cent and 36 per cent of first votes. A similar percentage of the second vote won them three (from 56) and one (from 20) regional seats in the respective elections. Under this system it is clear therefore that to gain an overall majority, a political party would probably need to increase its percentage of second votes. This system is not, of course, a truly proportional system but a hybrid born out of compromise. It goes some way to addressing the criticism that "the British electoral system permits minority rule"[18]

[18] I. Loveland, *Constitutional Law: A Critical Introduction* (London: Butterworths, 1996) 277.

but in both Scotland and in Wales Labour won less than 40 per cent of the votes cast both for constituency and regional seats. Furthermore in Scotland the need to find a coalition partner brings into government a political party that received only 14 per cent and 13 per cent of the two votes. The influence of the Liberal Democratic Party in Scotland is therefore out of all proportion to its electoral support. In both cases, the Conservative party gained regional seats. The system therefore operated to their benefit. In the previous general election, the Conservative Party had won no seats at Westminster from Scottish constituencies.

The system of election used in Northern Ireland differs from that outlined above. Northern Ireland is divided into 18 constituencies and each voter has one single transferable vote. This system of proportional representation reflects practice in local elections in Northern Ireland. The use of proportional representation in Northern Ireland has long been accepted as a way of ensuring representation of both community traditions. It had been used, for example, in elections to the European Parliament.

The first elections to the New Northern Ireland Assembly took place on June 25, 1998. The results were as follows[19]:

Party	Seats
Ulster Unionist Party	28
Social Democratic and Labour Party	24
Democratic Unionist Party	20
Sinn Fein	18
The Alliance Party	6
★Northern Ireland Unionist Party	4
★★United Unionist Assembly Party	3
Northern Ireland Women's Coalition	2
Progressive Unionist Party	2
UK Unionist Party	1
★★★Independent Unionist	1

- ★ Elected as UK Unionist Party, resigned and formed new party with effect from January 15, 1999.
- ★★ Elected as Independents and formed UUAP September 21, 1998

[19] These results are taken from http://www.ni-assembly.gov.uk/parties.htm

- *** Member expelled from NIUP December 2, 1999.

This system produced a balance of representation broadly in line with the sizes of the two community traditions in Northern Ireland. The unionists gained the majority of seats but the republicans form a large minority.

It is clear that the different systems of elections used for the devolved parliamentary bodies is the result of political compromise. In Northern Ireland, without proportional representation, whole sections of the community would consider themselves to be disenfranchised. A well-known system was therefore continued. In Scotland and Wales, proportional representation in any form was new. New Labour had, however, particularly in its relationship with the Liberal Democratic Party, agreed to throw off its traditional hostility to proportional representation, at least as far as the new devolved institutions was concerned. However there was not, and there still is not, complete acceptance of the principle of proportional representation within the Labour Party. Hence the compromise and hence the reason why the Northern Irish system was not borrowed and used in all three elections. There is no legal reason why one system would be chosen over the other but it may seem odd that the Scottish Parliament and the Northern Ireland Assembly that share similar functions should not be elected in the same way. The National Assembly for Wales, by contrast, has very different functions from the Scottish Parliament but shares a method of election.

It is entirely possible to live with different types of electoral systems within the United Kingdom. In Europe, there are even different electoral systems for the one European Parliament. However, there is a danger of confusing the electorate with different systems. On the day of the first elections to the Scottish Parliament local government elections were also being held using the first past the post system. Each elector had three votes to play with and the effect of casting each of these three votes was different. This is unsatisfactory, particularly coupled with the fact that some five weeks later, elections to the European Parliament were held using an entirely different system. If the aim of constitutional reform is to connect people back to politics then one aspect of a modern system must be that it should be comprehensible and straightforward. There seems to be no clear vision within New Labour of what a "modern" electoral system might be like. It is difficult (perhaps impossible) to think of any other constitutional model where the basis of the electoral system differs from one regional government to another.

Members interests and conduct

In the minds of the public the words corruption and politician have often been intertwined. In recent years there have been several attempts to ensure that the conduct of elected representatives meets acceptable standards. Two issues might be distinguished. The first relates to the requirement that an elected representative should not participate in decision making where his/her own pecuniary interests are affected. The second relates to the need for politicians to be free from undue influence in their work. The Local Government Act 1972 (c.70 sections 94 and 98) for England and Wales and the Local Government (Scotland) Act 1973 (c.65 section 38) required members of local authorities to disclose any pecuniary interest in a contract which was under discussion. He/she thereafter could not take part in discussions nor vote on the award of the contract. A record of such disclosures was to be maintained by the local authority concerned. Breach of these provisions might lead to a criminal penalty. The Local Government and Housing Act 1989 went further (c.42). This Act, which applies in this respect to England, Wales and Scotland, requires councillors to provide details of pecuniary interests to be kept in a register open to the public. Failure to comply is a criminal offence. In addition, a national code of conduct for councillors was adopted on the basis of section 31 of that Act which all councillors must accept on taking up office. Local government politicians are therefore subject to a mixture of self- regulation and the ultimate sanction of the criminal law.[20]

The House of Commons by contrast regulates its own pro-cedures.[21] Members were first required to register their interests in 1975 but a number of scandals led to the establishment of a standing

---

[20] The Local Government Bill currently before Parliament allows the Secretary of State (for England) and the National Assembly for Wales (for Wales) to specify the principles which are to govern the conduct of members and co-opted members of relevant authorities. These principles may be specified in a code and a duty is imposed on relevant authorities to adopt a code if an Order is made requiring them to do so. A person who becomes a member or is co-opted to membership of an authority has a duty to comply with the code of conduct. Standards committees are to be established to police the operation of the code of conduct. The Ethical Standards in Public Life Bill currently before the Scottish Parliament makes similar provision in respect of authorities in Scotland.

[21] Although there are now proposals to extend the law on bribery to cover MPs. See *Reinforcing Standards: Sixth Report of the Committee on Standards in Public Life* Cm 4557-I (2000) where this proposal is endorsed.

committee to investigate standards in public life. The Nolan Committee Report of 1995 led to the introduction of more stringent measures.[22] The Parliamentary Commissioner for Standards was appointed to maintain the register of members' interests and gives advice on its interpretation. The Register is open to public inspection. The Select Committee on Standards and Privileges was established to consider matters referred from the Commissioner and a Code of Conduct was adopted regulating the behaviour of Members of the House of Commons.[23] The Select Committee on Standards and Privileges recommended a ban on paid advocacy. Members of Parliament may not accept remuneration "to advocate or initiate any cause or matter on behalf of any outside body or individual" or urge other Members to do so.[24]

Many of the lessons learned from Westminster have been translated into legislative form for the devolved institutions. Throughout the work of the Consultative Steering Group for the Scottish Parliament and the National Assembly Advisory Group in Wales, there is a strong thread that devolution should bring about a new politics based on principles of openness, inclusiveness and integrity. It was hoped that allegations of sleaze could not be levelled at the new institutions. In the devolution settlements, there is a mixture of statutory and non-statutory provisions so that, for example, the Scottish Parliament is required to ensure that there is a Register of Members' interests but it can develop it own codes of conduct based on standing orders. There is also a mixture of enforcement techniques based on parliamentary procedures backed up, in some circumstances, by the criminal law. The use of criminal penalties is reminiscent of the regulation of members of local authorities.

It is in Scotland where the rules on Members' conduct and interest are best articulated. The Northern Ireland Assembly is in the process of developing its own codes—delay on these matters being inevitable during the period of suspension. The National Assembly for Wales has also adopted a code of practice for AMs but this code is not as full as that for Scotland. The emphasis here is on the Scottish approach with reference, where appropriate, to the other devolved institutions.

The Scotland Act provides that the Proceedings of the Parliament shall be regulated by standing orders.[25] It also requires that provision

---

[22] *First Report of the Committee on Standards in Public Life* Cm 2850 (1995).
[23] HC Deb vol . . . cols 610–612 November 6, 1995.
[24] *Second Report from the Select Committee on Standards in Public Life* HC 816 (1994–1995).
[25] Scotland Act, s.22.

be made for the registration of Members' interests and the prohibition of paid advocacy.[26] Contravention of the rules on paid advocacy or of the rules of participation in the proceedings of the Parliament without following the rules on registration of interests is made an offence. Provision in this section of the Act means a provision made by or under an Act of the Scottish Parliament. To date the Scottish Parliament has not made any such provision although the Parliament does intend to bring forward its own legislation covering these matters. In the meantime, provision has been made in respect of registration of interests and the prohibition of paid advocacy under the powers granted to the Secretary of State to make transitional arrangements for the Scottish Parliament.[27] Using the same powers the Secretary of State made the original standing orders of the Scottish Parliament[28] but these have now been replaced by standing orders made under section 22 and adopted by a Resolution of the Parliament of December 9, 1999 and came into force December 17, 1999.[29] These standing orders provide that the Scottish Parliament may adopt a Code of Conduct for MSPs and such a code was agreed by resolution of the Parliament on February 24, 2000 and came into force immediately.[30]

The Code is a mixture of statutory and non-statutory rules as well as advice and commentary on these rules. It is based on the work of the Code of Conduct Working Group of the CSG and is stated to be consistent with the principles set out in the Nolan Committee Report of 1995. The Code covers the registration and declaration of Members interests, rules relating to paid advocacy, the registration of interests of Members' staff, the rules on cross-party groups and rules governing the conduct of members in the chamber and in committee. It is policed by the Standards Committee of the Scottish Parliament whose remit includes considering and reporting on whether a Member has complied with the Code or any other rules and recommending, as appropriate, whether the rights and privileges of any MSP should be suspended.

---

[26] Scotland Act, s.39.
[27] Scotland Act, ss.112(1), 113 and 129(1). Under these powers the Secretary of State made S.I. 1999/1350 the Scotland Act 1998 (Transitory and Transitional Provisions) (Members' Interests) Order 1999 which came into force June 4, 1999.
[28] S.I. 1999/1095 the Scotland Act 1998 (Transitory and Transitional Provisions) (Standing Orders and Parliamentary Publications) Order 1999 which came into force May 6, 1999.
[29] They can be found at http://www.scottish.parliament.uk/parl_bus/sto1.htm
[30] It can be found at http:www.scottish.parliament.uk/msps/coc/coc-c.htm

The Scottish Code borrows six of the seven principles of public life recommended by Nolan—the principle of objectivity is omitted.[31] Two additional principles are added, public duty and duty as a representative. The public duty is expressed in terms of the duty to act in the interests of the Scottish people and the Scottish Parliament, to uphold the law and to bear allegiance to the Queen. The duty of a representative is to be accessible to the people of the area for which they have been elected and to represent their interests whilst respecting individual privacy. Accessibility was a key element of the work of the CSG and is intended to mark out the Scottish Parliament as an institution that is open to the public rather than as an institution that is responsive to the needs of selected interest groups. This issue came to the fore in September 1999 when it was alleged that certain lobbyists claimed to be able to have access to the diaries of certain members of the Scottish Executive and to have influence over them. The Standards Committee investigated these allegations and declared them to be unfounded.[32]

The Code goes on to explain the importance of the Members Interests Order.[33] The Order establishes a Register of Interests and provides the details that must be provided. The register is published on the Internet and is modelled on the register that is used in Westminster. An MSP who does not comply with the rules outlined

---

[31] The National Assembly for Wales Code of Standards for Members is a much shorter document than the Scottish Code (two pages as against 91). It borrows the seven Nolan principles directly but adds the principle of public duty. In Wales this principle is expressed in terms of a duty to uphold the law and in accordance with the public trust placed in them. They have a general duty to act in the interests of Wales and a special duty to the residents of the area for which they have been elected. Thus in Wales the duty of a representative is subsumed in the general public duty.

[32] The terms of reference of the investigation are found in Standards Committee Minutes, Sixth Meeting, Session 1 (1999) Tuesday October 5, 1999 and the hearings are recorded in the Minutes of the following meetings.

[33] The equivalent Welsh provisions are found in the Standing Orders for the National Assembly for Wales made by the Secretary of State for Wales under s.50(3) of the Government of Wales Act. These standing orders will remain in force unless and until they are remade by the Assembly. S.72 of the Government of Wales Act requires standing orders to include provision for the registration and declaration of Members' interests. In Northern Ireland standing orders must be made, amended or repealed by the Northern Ireland Assembly with cross-community support. They must provide for a register of Members' interests and rules on declaration of interests (s.43). The Northern Ireland approach (rules must be provided for in standing orders) mirrors that of the National Assembly for Wales whereas in Scotland provision must be made in or under Scottish legislation. The effect is the same, however, there must be provision in relation to Members' interests and violation of the rules is an offence.

in the Order in relation to registration of his/her interests may be suspended from proceedings in Parliament on a motion from the Standards Committee and may also be guilty of an offence. One way of avoiding confusion over the meaning of the Order is to provide guidelines and explanation as to its meaning and the Code of Conduct does this. For example, the Code of Conduct reminds MSPs that the definition of sponsorship includes receiving "any financial or material support on a continuing basis from any person to assist him or her as a member".[34] The Standards Committee took the view that Lord Watson had received sponsorship in accepting assistance to prepare the Protection of Wild mammals Bill which would outlaw hunting with hounds in Scotland. He had therefore a registrable interest. Failure to register such an interest did not, however, give rise to a right on the part of a member of the public to bring proceedings for interdict against Lord Watson.[35] In coming to this conclusion The Lord President observed that sanctions for breach of the Order were intended to be retrospective so that "they bite only, and not before, the breach takes place". This is very much line with the practice at Westminster. The difference between the two approaches being, of course, that there is no criminal penalty that might attach to a breach of the House of Commons procedure whereas there is a criminal penalty that might attach to a breach of the Scottish Order. It would be for the Procurator Fiscal in Scotland to bring any such criminal charge.

Before participating in the proceedings of the Scottish Parliament, a Member who has a registrable interest and that "interest would prejudice or might be thought by others to prejudice the member's ability to take part in proceedings in a disinterested way" must make an oral declaration of such an interest. Such an interest in known as a declarable interest. Any Member who wishes to speak on a matter in which he/she has a declarable interest must make a declaration. This is a statutory requirement but the Code also states that it is good practice for Members to provide a written declaration of relevant interest when lodging any written notice, *e.g.* when lodging a parliamentary question. Breach of these rules might result in a penalty being imposed by the Standards Committee or may constitute a criminal offence.

---

[34] Para. 4.3.22.
[35] *Whaley v. Lord Watson of Invergowrie* [2000] SLT 475.

As is the case with Westminster, paid advocacy is not permitted. However, the prohibition in not in the same terms. In 1995, the House of Commons agreed that "no Member shall, in consideration of any remuneration . . . advocate or initiate any cause or matter on behalf of any outside body or individual". This was the response of the House to the "cash for questions" scandal. The Scottish rule, in Article 6 of the Order, is much more prescriptive. It states that an MSP who receives or expects to receive any remuneration shall not "do anything in his capacity as a member in any proceedings which relates directly to the affairs or interests of, or which seek to confer benefit upon, the person from whom the Member received or expects to receive remuneration or to the affairs and interests of a client or an associate of that person". There is no mention in the Scottish version of intention—in consideration of—but instead there is a blanket ban. On a literal meaning a dentist, who intended to return to work as dentist after being an MSP, could not participate in proceedings in Parliament where dental matters were being discussed.

The Code of Conduct ignores the difference in wording and states that the crucial issue is intention. It states "the purpose of the rule is to prevent a member advocating any cause **in consideration of** any remuneration" (emphasis in original).[36] The Code goes on to say that the prohibition on paid advocacy does not prevent a Member engaging in paid work, or from being sponsored by an organisation or from holding a registrable interest. A literal reading would, however, place a ban on any MSP from participating in any activity of the Parliament where his/her employment or sponsorship relates directly to the interests of the employer or sponsor. Given that the Code does not have statutory force, MSPs might best be warned to follow the literal meaning of the Order to avoid possible criminal sanctions. This may be an area where the Scottish Parliament ought to consider legislation to clarify any possible confusion between the rules.

A potential overlap with the problem of paid advocacy is the abuse of the system of cross-party groups. To avoid such abuse, the House of Commons has put in place "a number of measures to increase the transparency of the operation of these groups" including an Approved list and a register of Members.[37] This issue has not been

---

[36] Para. 6.2.3.
[37] *Reinforcing Standards: Sixth Report of the Committee on Standards in Public Life* Cm 4557–I (2000) para. 7.58.

dealt with by legislation but the Code of Conduct seeks to regulate the activities of cross-party groups. These are defined as groups that "contain members from across the parties who share an interest in a particular subject or cause and they may include people from outwith the Parliament".[38] A potential cross-party group must apply to the Standards Committee for recognition. Detailed rules are set out in the Code relating to composition and purpose and the information that must be provided to enable the Standards Committee to reach a judgement on an application. The purpose of these rules is to ensure transparency in the operation of cross-party groups.

It is clear that the rules applicable to the conduct of MSPs have been based on experience at Westminster. There has been an attempt to prevent the repetition of any of the problems that arose in Westminster in relation to the failure to meet high standards of integrity in public life. Statutory regulation, backed up with the possible sanction of the use of the criminal law, goes some way to ensuring that the devolved institutions will not meet with the same problems and rigorous self regulation by Standards Committees would do the rest. In this respect all three of the devolved institutions will be operating to roughly the same standards.

Cross-community consent—designation of political identity

An arrangement which is unique to the Northern Ireland Assembly is the method of voting on certain key issues. In negotiating the Belfast Agreement care was taken to ensure that on key issues cross-community support was required. Thus the Northern Ireland Assembly requires cross-community support for the election of the Presiding Officer, for making or amending standing orders, making of or voting on resolutions relating to financial acts of the Assembly and for the adoption of the draft budget.[39] Cross community support is also required for the election of the First Minister and Deputy First Minister although in this case the Act specifies that for this election parallel consent is required.[40] Parallel consent needs a

---

[38] Para. 8.1.1.
[39] Northern Ireland Act, ss.39(7), 41, 63, 64.
[40] Northern Ireland Act, s.16(3).

majority of members present and voting including a majority of those designated unionist or nationalist. Cross community support can also be evidenced by weighted majority. Weighted majority means 60 per cent of members present and voting including at least 40 per cent of the nationalist and unionist designations present and voting. To organise this system it is necessary that Members of the Northern Ireland Assembly register a "designation of identity" at the first meeting of the Assembly. They must register whether they are unionist, nationalist or other for the purposes of certain votes.[41] These rules have no equivalent in either the Scottish or the Welsh settlements.

Committees

The White Papers setting out the government's views on the new devolved institutions stressed the need for them to adopt best and modern working practices reflecting principles of openness, accountability and inclusiveness. A great deal of emphasis was placed on the need for a strong committee structure reflecting the needs of a modern parliamentary institution. It was anticipated that the bulk of the work of the parliamentary bodies would be conducted through committees. This section examines these committee structures since it is in their operation that the devolved institutions are self-consciously "modern".

Different types of committees are required in the legislation. There is a broad pattern common to the three institutions. Statutory or subject committees are created in areas where powers have been transferred to the devolved institutions. Mandatory committees exist to regulate the internal workings of the parliamentary body or to co-ordinate policy.

Statutory or subject committees

The Northern Ireland Act provides for the establishment of "statutory" committees to "advise and assist each Northern Ireland

---

[41] The rules are found in the Preliminary Arrangements under the Standing Orders of the Northern Ireland Assembly. They can be found on http://www.ni-assembly.gov.uk/standing orders.htm

Minister in the formulation of policy".[42] The powers of the statutory committees were determined during the multi-party negotiations and are set out in the Belfast Agreement. They have "a scrutiny, development and consultation role".[43] They also have the power to initiate legislation. Their powers are listed in the Belfast Agreement as follows. They can consider and advise on departmental plans, including budgets, approve relevant secondary legislation and take the committee stage of primary legislation, call for persons and papers, initiate enquiries and make reports and consider and advise on matters brought to the committee by the relevant Minister. The subject committee cannot be chaired by a member of the same political party as the Minister. This means that responsibility for a particular devolved area is shared between the political parties. For example, the Minister responsible for Education in Northern Ireland is Martin McGuinness of Sinn Fein. The Convener of the statutory committee is Mr Kennedy of the Ulster Unionist Party and the Deputy Chair is Sam Wilson of the Democratic Unionists. Thus power is shared in the area of education between the two communities. This system is intended to guard against any abuse of power by one of the political parties or communities. Ministerial posts are allocated on the basis of the d'Hondt system[44] as are committee chairs and vice-chairs. Again this is an attempt to ensure power sharing between the two communities.

The Scotland Act is largely silent on the functions and structure of committees that should be established although it is clear that the use of such committees is envisaged since committees are given extensive powers to call for witnesses and documents. Standing Orders, however, distinguish subject committees and mandatory committees. Subject committees are the equivalent of statutory committees in Northern Ireland. The functions of subject committees are laid down in Standing Orders. They are in similar terms to Northern Irish statutory committees. Subject committees may examine any competent matter, conduct relevant inquiries, consider the policy and administration of the Scottish Administration, consider proposals for secondary or primary legislation whether before the Scottish Parliament or the United Kingdom Parliament, consider any relevant European legislation or international obligation, consider the need for

---

[42] Northern Ireland Act, s.29.
[43] *Agreement reached in multi-party negotiations* Cm 4292 (1998), Strand One.
[44] See Chapter 4 below.

law reform, initiate Bills and consider any financial proposals relating to any relevant matter.[45]

The Government of Wales Act uses the term statutory committees to include subject committees and other specified committees.[46] Subject committees have responsibilities in the fields in which the Assembly has functions.[47] There must be the same number of subject committees as there are Assembly Secretaries to whom the First Secretary has allocated responsibility for a particular subject matter.[48] That Assembly Secretary becomes a member of the subject committee. The functions of the subject committees are set out in standing orders. They are to contribute to the development of the Assembly's policies, to keep under review the expenditure and administration of the Assembly's policies and to keep under review the discharge of public functions in those fields.[49] They may also advise on proposed legislation affecting Wales, provide advice to the Assembly Cabinet on budgetary matters, investigate complaints, review public appointments and consider matters referred by the Assembly.

The work of the subject committees in the three parliamentary institutions can be examined from at least five different perspectives: the scrutiny and revision of legislation, a role in policy formulation, a role in initiation of legislation, a role in ensuring accountability of the executive and as a mechanism of increasing transparency in the work of the devolved bodies.

The Scottish Parliament and the Northern Ireland Assembly are unicameral legislatures. There is no revising chamber for the primary legislation that is made by these parliaments. There is a need, therefore, to ensure that revision and scrutiny of legislation is carried out during the legislative process and it is here that the subject committees have a key role. A Bill is allocated to a lead subject committee for the second stage in the legislative process. This is the detailed scrutiny of new legislation.[50] In the Scottish Parliament and the Northern Ireland Assembly subject committees fulfil the revising function of the House of Lords.

---

[45] Rule 6.2.
[46] Government of Wales Act, ss.56–61.
[47] Government of Wales Act, s.57.
[48] See Chapter 4 below.
[49] Rule 9.8.
[50] See Chapter 3 below for a description of these processes.

Subject committees have a role in policy formulation. This is most clearly articulated in the National Assembly for Wales and the Northern Ireland Assembly. In Wales, the relevant Assembly Secretary is a member of the subject committee that mirrors his/her area of accountability. The role of the subject committee is specifically stated in terms of contribution to the policy of the Assembly. The statutory committees of the Northern Ireland Assembly are given a similar role in that they are a mechanism for power sharing. Although a Minister is responsible for an area of policy, he/she must work with the committees who advise and assist in the formulation of policy. The subject committees of the Scottish Parliament play a more reactive role than this. They may consider and report on the policy of the Scottish Executive and thereby influence that policy but they are not given a direct role in policy formulation equivalent to that seen in the Irish and Welsh settlements.

Subject committees in Northern Ireland and in Scotland may initiate legislation. Such legislation is likely to arise out of the longer term working of the committees. Once they have developed expertise, they are more likely to be in a position to recognise the need for legislation. In the first year of the Scottish Parliament there have been no proposals for legislation from committees.

The use of committees to investigate and scrutinise the work of the executive is well developed in Westminster. In terms of accountability, however, the devolution settlements differ from the Westminster model. Accountability issues are dealt with in a different manner.[51] None the less subject committees do have an important role in probing and discussing the administration of the relevant devolved executives. They have powers to call for witnesses and papers so that the work of the regional governments can be brought into the open and put under public scrutiny. Thus the aim of increasing transparency in decision making at the local level is increased.

Mandatory committees

In addition to these subject committees there are a number of mandatory (Scotland) or statutory (Wales) committees that have been

---

[51] These issues are dealt with in more depth in the following chapter.

established to regulate the work of the parliamentary bodies. The Standards Committee has been discussed above but there are also committees to regulate procedures, to scrutinise secondary legislation, to monitor European legislation and policy. Both institutions also have equal opportunities committees and the Scottish Parliament has a Petitions Committee which can receive public petitions in the form of suggestions for legislation or in the form of complaints.

Business committees

A parliamentary bureau or business committee is a well known feature of several European parliaments and of the European Parliament. It is designed to ensure that the interests of all the political groupings are taken into account when deciding on priorities. The use of the business committee is intended to reflect a modern parliament by creating a forum in which deals are done and rules developed. This is in contrast to the more "usual channels" where business is conducted in the House of Commons. Business committees have been established in all three devolved parliamentary institutions.

The Parliamentary Bureau of the Scottish Parliament proposes the daily and weekly business programmes, proposes the establishment, composition and remit of committees and time-tables debates. It consists of the Presiding Officer and representatives of the main political parties. The equivalent to the Scottish Parliamentary Bureau in Wales is the Business Committee although its powers are very much more attenuated than those of the former body. This is because the Assembly Business Secretary, who is a member of the Assembly Cabinet, determines the business of the Assembly. The function of the Business Committee is, therefore, advisory. The Business Committee can advise the Assembly Business Secretary on the management of the Assembly's functions and the Deputy on the exercise of his/her functions or the procedures to be used in the adoption of delegated legislation. It may also make recommendations to the Assembly on procedural matters, including recommendations on revision of Standing Orders. Like the Scottish Parliamentary Bureau, the Business Committee is composed of a member from each political group. A Business Committee also exists in the Northern Ireland Assembly. It has similar functions to the Scottish Parliamentary Bureau but many of its procedures are laid down in the legislation and are conducted in public. For example, the running of the d'Hondt formula for the choice of committee convenerships was done within the Assembly itself whereas in Scotland this was done in the secrecy of the Parliamentary Bureau.

Regional committees

Regional committees are unique to the Welsh settlement. They are a form of reassurance that the interest of one part of Wales will not override the interests of the others. There are, of course, several divisions in Wales. North and South Wales, English and Welsh speaking Wales, the richer East Wales against the poorer West Wales. These divisions were mirrored in the results of the referendum on devolution. Support for devolution was strongest in the economically less advanced West Wales than in the richer regions bordering England. In fact the "yes" vote coincided almost completely with the Objective I status map recently adopted under the European Commission structural funding arrangements.[52]

The Government of Wales Act specifies that there must be a Committee for North Wales and committees for other regions but leaves the definition of boundaries to be dealt with by Standing Orders. The National Assembly Advisory Group (NAAG) found that the definition of the boundaries of the regional committees was one of its most difficult tasks with at least one commentator criticising each option that the NAAG examined. At the end of the consultation period NAAG suggested the establishment of four regional committees but recognised that the boundaries may have to be changed by the Assembly given that there was no perfect solution to the boundary question. As it stands, the solution adopted in Standing Orders means that there is not absolute correspondence between the regional committee boundaries and the boundaries of the new economic regions in Wales nor of the unitary health authority boundaries.

These regional committees are advisory only and are made up of the Members representing the constituency and electoral regions falling within the areas outlined above. For this reason there is no

---

[52] This point was made by Barry Jones in a paper given at the conference on *Devolution—the European Dimension* in Ballycastle June 17–18, 1999.

requirement that they reflect the political balance in the Assembly.[53] Their function is to advise the Assembly on matters relating to their region and on the impact of Assembly policies in that region. Meetings will take place twice a year within the region. NAAG recommended that the regional committee should come to an understanding with local authorities to examine how they might usefully co-operate and also recommends that the meetings of the regional committees might take place in premises provided by local authorities. The first meetings of the regional committees did in fact take place in the offices of local authorities. NAAG saw the regional committees as being the "part of the Assembly structure that is perceived as being closest to the people and local areas of Wales". It remains to be seen how the committees will work with the Assembly and whether they will encroach on the functions of local authorities.

The committees of the Scottish Parliament and the National Assembly for Wales have been operating for only a matter of months and the committees of the Northern Irish Assembly were no sooner established than suspended. It is therefore difficult to draw any firm conclusions. In his study of the operation of the first six months of the National Assembly for Wales, Osmond raises several interesting issues in relation to the operation of the committees there.[54] He concludes that in the first six months, the committee members have been on a steep learning curve. They have had to come to grips with a large volume of briefing and background paper to read into their new roles. Given that much of this information is controlled by the executive and it is sometimes passed to the committees at a very late stage this means that the executive has been able to control the committees or at least avoid rigorous and searching scrutiny.[55] However, Osmond notes a couple of occasions where committee chairs have been effective in holding the executive to account. Cynog Dafis was able to force a full examination on the proposals of the

---

[53] In both the Scottish Parliament and the National Assembly for Wales for there is a requirement that parties are allocated seats on committees in relation to their party strength. This means that in the Scottish Parliament the Labour Party/Liberal Democratic coalition always has a majority whereas in Wales the Labour Party is always in the minority.

[54] J. Osmond, *Devolution: A dynamic, settled process?* (Cardiff: Institute for Welsh Affairs, 1999).

[55] Control of information by the Scottish Executive has been noted by A. Wilson, "Modernising the Scottish Parliament" in G. Hassan and C. Warhurst (eds), *A Different Future: a Modernisers' Guide to Scotland* (Glasgow: The Big Issue in Scotland, 1999).

Education and Training Action Group. Ron Davies, given his prior knowledge of Welsh Office spending, was able to force a debate on the Treasury withholding matching funding for European Objective I investment. Osmond believes that it is easier for committees to make their mark where the chair is a member of an opposition party. On a more worrying note, he cites the exchange between the Liberal Democrat leader, Mike German, and Alun Michael over the effect of a negative vote of a subject committee. In the debate the Assembly Secretary stated that the views of subject committees had no more weight than any other party consulted on a particular issue.

There is no equivalent Scottish study to this. However some of Omond's conclusions can be applied to the committees of the Scottish Parliament. Members of these committees have also been on a steep learning curve with the staff of the Scottish Parliament being inundated with requests for information and briefing. The result is that the committees have begun to prioritise their work as they begin to understand their role. There has also been conflict between the committees and the Scottish Executive over the extent to which the committees have a right to question Ministers. In response to heavy questioning of the Health Minister in committee it was reported that new protocols would be introduced requiring prior notice of questions. Some committee chairs opposed the proposals which have not yet been published.[56]

Comparing the parliamentary institutions

It will become clear in the following chapter that the three parliamentary institutions are allocated different functions. It might be expected that the difference in functions might explain the differences in structure between them. This is not the case. The difference in structure results from the difference in the political bargains made about devolution in each region. The structure and many of the rules governing the Northern Ireland Assembly is a result of the agreements made during the negotiations leading to the Belfast Agreement. The size of the Assembly, the degree of proportional representation, the manner in which committees are established are unique to the Northern Ireland Assembly. The same can

---

[56] *The Herald*, November 25. 1999.

be said for the Scottish Parliament and the National Assembly for Wales. Each has its own idiosyncratic structure. Thus although the Government of Wales Act and the Scotland Act both distinguish constituency and regional members and the method of election is the same the degree of proportionality is different. The greater influence of the Liberal Democrats in Scotland results from their long-standing commitment to devolution and their determination in the Scottish Constitutional Convention to hold out for proportional representation.

Some aspects are common and these are based on Westminster practices. The regulation of Members' interests and the need to provide systems to ensure high standards in public life have led to the introduction of fairly stringent controls based on Westminster practices but backed up by the use of criminal penalties in many instances. Thus the regulation of the devolved institutions is not left entirely to the parliamentary bodies themselves.

The importance of subject committees—despite the differences between them in terms of functions—is another common theme. Subject committees are seen as a way of sharing power between the parliamentary bodies and the executive and as a way of ensuring that the executives are accountable ultimately to the people in the region. The committees of each parliamentary body will need time to bed down and to develop an understanding of their role. A possible future development might be inter-parliamentary co-operation on matters of common concern. Chapter 5 of this book discusses "intra-governmental co-operation" where there are clear mechanisms for executive level co-operation. These mechanisms are not replicated as yet at the level of the parliamentary bodies yet such co-operation might become essential if the regional executives are really to be held accountable for their own actions within the intra-governmental sphere.

Chapter 3

Parliamentary functions

Introduction

This chapter examines two of the main functions of the parliamentary institutions established under devolution; the power to legislate and the power to hold the newly created executives to account. In particular, it describes the differences between the three devolution settlements. The power to legislate and the power to scrutinise the executive are two functions that are common to most parliamentary institutions in western democracies. The power to adopt primary legislation is shared by the Scottish Parliament and the Northern Ireland Assembly. The National Assembly for Wales has a right to be consulted on Welsh primary legislation but does not have power of its own to adopt primary legislation. The extent of legislative competence differs between the Scottish Parliament and the Northern Ireland Assembly. Specific rules protecting human rights and cross community interests are written into the procedures of the Northern Ireland Assembly that are absent elsewhere.

The power to scrutinise the executives also differs between the three settlements. Again the National Assembly for Wales is the institution which is the furthest from the model of a true Parliament. As is explained below, the National Assembly for Wales is the executive and within it there is a delegation of powers to specific AMs known as Assembly Secretaries under the leadership of the First Secretary. In these circumstances, principles of accountability and techniques of scrutiny differ from that which is commonly understood in United Kingdom constitutional law and practice. In Northern Ireland, the legislation requires a level of personal commitment from the executive to the principles contained in the Belfast Agreement. The Northern Ireland Assembly has additional powers to hold Ministers to account in respect of these principles. The Scottish model of accountability and scrutiny of members of the Executive is more familiar. This is a system based on recognisable concepts of ministerial responsibility as this is traditionally understood in United Kingdom constitutional law.

Certain techniques are common to the three institutions in terms of methods of holding the executive branch to account and these methods are not discussed in this chapter. They are predictable. In Scotland, Wales and Northern Ireland the parliamentary institutions conduct debates. Members table written and oral questions. Members of the executive can be called to give evidence before committees. The chapter concentrates on the model of accountability to attempt to bring out the very real differences between the functions of the "parliamentary" institutions.

Power to legislate

Both the Scottish Parliament and the Northern Ireland Assembly have the power to make laws termed, in both cases, Acts.[1] Neither the Scotland Act nor the Northern Ireland Act provides a definition of this term. Nor does the legislation define the term "laws". This is not surprising since there is no general definition of either term in United Kingdom constitutional law. However, a generally acknowledged distinction is drawn between primary legislation adopted as Acts of the United Kingdom Parliament following "a series of stages prescribed by Parliamentary Standing Orders"[2] and subordinate legislation (also termed secondary or delegated legislation). Subordinate legislation is defined in the Interpretation Act, 1978 as meaning "Orders in Council, orders, rules, regulations, schemes, warrants, bye-laws and other instruments made under any Act".[3] A more general definition can be given as legislation "drafted by government departments under rule making powers conferred on a Minister by an Act of Parliament".[4]

Thus in United Kingdom constitutional law there are two types of legislation, Acts of Parliament (primary legislation) and an assortment

---

[1] Scotland Act 1998, s.28: Northern Ireland Act 1998, s.5.
[2] A, Le Sueur, J. Herberg and R. English, *Principles of Public Law,* (2nd ed.) (London: Cavendish, 1999) at 125.
[3] Interpretation Act 1978 s.21.
[4] Le Sueur *et al.* in note 1, 127.

of rules made under various powers derived from an Act of Parliament (subordinate legislation). Where do Acts of the devolved legislatures fit into this scheme? Are such Acts a species of primary legislation or a species of subordinate legislation? Underlying this seemingly simple legal question is a deeply political argument about the nature of devolution itself. To recognise that the devolved legislatures have the power to adopt primary legislation is to acknowledge that a transfer has taken place from one legislature to another, albeit in limited fields. To qualify such legislation as subordinate is to equate the devolved legislatures with a government department or local authority to whom powers may be delegated at the behest of central government and equally easily removed. According to this latter interpretation, by enacting the Scotland Act and the Northern Ireland Act, Parliament has not *transferred* powers to but *conferred* powers on the devolved legislatures. To describe Scottish or Northern Irish legislation as subordinate would also mean that any Act of the United Kingdom would potentially trump any Act of the devolved legislatures, even if that Act was validly enacted and within devolved powers. Faced with a conflict between an Act of the United Kingdom Parliament and an Act of the devolved legislature, the courts would have to apply the former.

It can be argued that Acts of the devolved legislatures are a species of secondary legislation. Powers have been conferred on the Scottish Parliament and the Northern Ireland Assembly to make subordinate legislation. Bradley and Ewing state, for example, that there are instruments which "fall short of being an Act of Parliament" and therefore the courts will not attribute legislative supremacy to these acts.[5] Listed amongst those instruments that fall short in this way are acts of a subordinate legislature. In support of this view, Bradley and Ewing cite the case of *Belfast Corpn v. OD Cars Ltd*,[6] a case concerning the meaning to be given to definitions of property and compensation in planning legislation in force in Northern Ireland in the 1950s.

The Belfast Corporation case relates to the interpretation and definition of planning legislation adopted by the Northern Ireland Parliament in 1931 and 1944. In that case the House of Lords was asked to address the issue of whether the planning legislation was

---

[5] A. W. Bradley and K. D. Ewing, *Constitutional and Administrative Law* (12th ed.) (Harlow: Lonman, 1997) at 59.
[6] [1960] A.C. 490.

ultra vires the Government of Ireland Act, 1920. That Act specifically precluded the Northern Ireland Parliament from enacting legislation the effect of which would favour one religion over another. Their Lordships treated the issue as one of interpretation of the planning legislation and did not directly address the question of vires. Even if they had, the question would merely turn on whether the Northern Ireland Parliament had acted within its powers. The House of Lords was not invited to discuss the status of Northern Ireland legislation therefore no conclusion can be drawn from this case as to the status, quality or characteristics of the legislation adopted by the Northern Ireland Parliament.

The case is interesting, however, because the House of Lords heard arguments from the Attorney General for Northern Ireland, a United Kingdom government minister, about the nature of devolved powers. He argued that under section 4 of the Northern Ireland Act, 1920 legislative powers are "given" to the Northern Ireland Parliament and "so long as it keeps within its own field it is the master . . . The powers of the Northern Ireland Parliament should be construed widely so as to make it master in its own house".[7] He argued that wherever possible a construction should be given to avoid holding legislation to be ultra vires. The Attorney General was therefore clearly of the view that validly enacted legislation should not be subject to further review by the courts.

A second line of argument can be led in support of the view that Scottish or Northern Irish Acts are a species of subordinate legislation. The Human Rights Act 1998 defines subordinate legislation, for the purpose of the Act, to include an Act of the Scottish Parliament and an Act of the Northern Ireland Assembly.[8] The significance of this provision it that the courts may revoke any provision of subordinate legislation which is incompatible with the Human Rights Act but may only issue a declaration of incompatibility against primary legislation. Thus the first Act of the Scottish Parliament, the Mental Health (Public Safety and Appeals) (Scotland) Act 1999 has been challenged on the grounds of its incompatibility with the Human Rights Act. These provisions, however, must be seen in the context of devolution. The Scotland Act specifically states that it is outwith the legislative competence of the Parliament to legislate

---

[7] Per W. B. Maginess Q.C., Attorney-General for Northern Ireland, C. A. Nicholson Q.C. and J. K. Pringle as *amici curiae Belfast Corpn v. OD Cars Ltd* [1960] A.C. 490, 502.
[8] Human Rights Act 1988, s.21.

contrary to any of the Convention rights.[9] The Northern Ireland Act contains a similar provision.[10] As with other questions of vires, this is a matter for the courts to determine.[11] If the Human Rights Act had categorised Acts of the devolved legislatures as being primary legislation for the purpose of that Act there would have been a conflict between the procedures established under the various Acts. It is therefore in keeping with the scheme of devolution to categorise Acts adopted by the devolved legislatures in such a way as to subject them to the same procedures as exist for other questions relating to vires. To do this Acts of the devolved legislatures could not be categorised as primary legislation for the purposes of the Human Rights Act.

Furthermore, both the Scottish Parliament and the Northern Ireland Assembly are public authorities for the purposes of the Human Rights Act.[12] As such it is unlawful for either body to do anything that is incompatible with a Convention right. This rule includes the adoption of primary legislation. There is nothing surprising in the proposition that a parliament should be subject to the rule of law. As the Lord President stated "in many democracies . . . they [parliaments] owe their existence and powers to statute and are in various ways subject to the law and to the courts which act to uphold the law. The Scottish Parliament has simply joined that wider family of parliaments".[13] The fact that the devolved legislatures must act within the limits of their competence does not therefore mean that they do not have power to adopt primary legislation, provided always that they act within the limits of their competence.

There are strong arguments to suggest that the devolved legislatures do have the power to adopt primary legislation within the fields specified in the legislation and, consequently, that the power to legislate has been transferred. Primary legislation enacted by the devolved legislatures is however valid only when it is within the competence of the devolved legislature. In accepting this view there is no suggestion that the devolved legislatures are sovereign but they are, to borrow an earlier Attorney General's phrase, masters of their own house.

The first legal argument in support of this view, that Acts of the devolved legislatures are a species of primary legislation, arises from

---

[9] Scotland Act s.29(2)(d).
[10] Northern Ireland Act, s.6(2)(c).
[11] See Chapter 6 below.
[12] Human Rights Act, s.6.
[13] *Per* Lord Rodgers *Whaley v. Lord Watson of Invergowrie* [2000] SLT 475, 481.

the terminology used in the devolution legislation itself. That legislation clearly distinguishes Acts from subordinate legislation. An Act of the Scottish Parliament, for example, has legal force when a Bill has been passed by the Parliament and has received Royal Assent. Every Act of the Scottish Parliament thereafter "shall be judicially noticed" and applied by the courts.[14] Similar words are used in the Northern Ireland Act.[15] It cannot be mere coincidence that this terminology of Bill and Act, and a similarity of procedural rules relating to parliamentary procedure and the giving of Royal Assent is used in the devolution legislation. This is a mirror image of the concept of primary legislation as that concept is understood in United Kingdom constitutional law. Within the devolved sphere Acts of the devolved legislatures are primary legislation. This view is supported by the Government spokesperson on devolution in the House of Lords. In reply to a question on what arrangements have been made to monitor the effectiveness of functions devolved to the Scottish Parliament, Baroness Ramsay of Cartvale stated that the Scotland Act provided mechanisms "designed to ensure that all primary and secondary legislation passed by the Scottish Parliament is within its legislative competence".[16] The clear view of Government is therefore that validly enacted Acts of the devolved legislatures is indeed primary legislation.

The devolution legislation also draws the distinction between Acts and subordinate legislation. Subordinate legislation in the Scotland Act is given the same meaning as in the Interpretation Act quoted above but that definition is extended to include any instrument made under an Act of the Scottish Parliament.[17] The concept of Scottish or Northern Irish subordinate legislation is the same concept as that familiar in United Kingdom constitutional law. It is clear therefore that the devolution legislation draws the distinction between primary and secondary legislation and does not equate them. This pattern is consistent with previous attempts at devolution. The Interpretation Act as it was adopted in 1978 did not include Acts of the Northern Ireland Parliament in its definition of subordinate legislation. Furthermore, the Interpretation Act itself was only made to apply to Acts of the United Kingdom Parliament in so far as they affected

---

[14] Scotland Act, s.29.
[15] Northern Ireland Act, s.5.
[16] HL Deb vol 612 col 5 April 10, 2000.
[17] Scotland Act, s.126.

Northern Ireland. Legislation of the Northern Irish Parliament was subject to its own rules of interpretation.

The Scotland Act amends the Interpretation Act to insert a new section 23A.[18] It does so only as far as making sections 15 to 18 applicable to Acts of the Scottish Parliament. It does not amend the definition of subordinate legislation contained in section 21. It is clear that the United Kingdom Parliament could have made such an amendment if it was the intention of that Parliament not to transfer the power to enact primary legislation.

The devolution legislation therefore transfers powers to the Scottish Parliament and the Northern Ireland Assembly to enact primary legislation. These laws are "every bit as much law as Acts of the United Kingdom Parliament".[19] At the same time, the legislation specifically states that such a transfer is without prejudice to the power of the United Kingdom Parliament to legislate for Scotland[20] and Northern Ireland.[21] Thus the site of authority for primary legislation is shared. A problem may arise if both legislatures seek to occupy the legislative space and conflicts arise between two validly enacted laws in the same subject area but with conflicting provisions.

Arrangements have been put in place to try to avoid such a conflict. Pre- and post legislative scrutiny of provisions of the devolved legislatures are intended to ensure that each acts within the legislative competence laid down by the Westminster Parliament. No such scrutiny is available in relation to legislation adopted at Westminster. Instead, devolution is safeguarded by a number of different devices.

In the case of Northern Ireland, the Northern Ireland Act gives to the Assembly the power to modify any provision made by or under an Act of Parliament in so far as it is part of the law of Northern Ireland.[22] Scottish legislation may similarly modify or repeal existing United Kingdom legislation. It may be counter-argued that the United Kingdom Parliament could continue to legislate so as to attempt to overrule the devolved legislatures leading to what has been described elsewhere as "legislative ping pong".[23] The House of

---

[18] Scotland Act, Sched 8.
[19] A. Page, C. Reid and A. Ross, *A Guide to the Scotland Act 1998* (Edinburgh; Butterworths, 1999) at 45.
[20] Scotland Act, s.28(7).
[21] Northern Ireland Act, s.6.
[22] Northern Ireland Act s.6.
[23] A. Page, C. Reid and A. Ross, *A Guide to the Scotland Act 1998* (Edinburgh; Butterworths, 1999) at 55.

Commons Select Committee on procedure addressed this problem.[24] It recommended the acceptance of certain general principles based on the recognition that "the Scottish Parliament will have powers to make its own primary legislation". The Committee stated that in passing the devolution legislation "Parliament has agreed that certain powers and responsibilities shall pass from it to the devolved legislatures" and as a result Parliament should not use its own procedures or customs to thwart this transfer.[25] In its report the Committee also agreed with the Government when it stated that it expected "that a convention would be adopted that Westminster would not normally legislate with regard to devolved matters without the consent of the devolved body". In supporting this statement the Committee agreed that "the House should not legislate on devolved matters without the consent of the legislature concerned".[26]

Thus a convention is being developed that Westminster will not legislate on any devolved matter without the consent of the relevant legislature. To enable this convention to operate, United Kingdom government departments will have to ensure pre-legislative scrutiny to ensure that the boundary between devolved and non-devolved matters is adequately policed. Further conventions need to be developed as to how the consent of the relevant legislature will be given if it is deemed necessary for Westminster to legislate for Scotland or Northern Ireland on any matter where power has been transferred. Donald Dewar has explained his view to the Scottish Parliament.[27] He stated that "where the Scottish Executive and the United Kingdom Government agree" that Westminster should legislate in a devolved area "it would be for Scottish Ministers to put the proposal to the Scottish Parliament". Thus a two-stage process is envisaged. First an agreement between governments must be reached and then approval by the devolved legislature is required.

These arrangements rely on goodwill. They are based on constitutional conventions rather than on constitutional guarantees. It might be argued that this is the inevitable outcome of the choice of devolution rather than the adoption of a federal system based on a formally guaranteed division of powers. It does mean however that

---

[24] HC *Select Committee on Procedure, Fourth Report.*

[25] *Fourth Report,* para. 5.

[26] *Fourth Report,* para. 26.

[27] Discussed in HC Research Paper 99/85 *The Procedural Consequences of Devolution* October 20, 1999, 21–23.

there is a possibility that conflicting legislation may be adopted and the courts will be faced with the requirement to apply two conflicting but equally valid provisions contained in primary legislation, the first in an Act of the United Kingdom Parliament and the second in an Act of a devolved legislature.

Faced with such a problem the first approach taken by the courts will be to attempt to reconcile the legislation using classic interpretation techniques and with due regard to the devolution legislation. This legislation however is more concerned with interpretation of Scottish or Northern Irish legislation on the question of competence rather than addressing the problem of conflicting legislation. Thus the Scotland Act requires the courts to adopt a purposive interpretation of a provision of an Act of the Scottish Parliament to determine whether it relates to a devolved matter.[28] The courts must have regard in determining this question to the effect of the provision "in all the circumstances". The courts are also required to police the boundary between matters which potentially straddle reserved and non-reserved matters. In these circumstances, the court must treat the matter as being reserved (*i.e.* a matter for the United Kingdom Parliament) unless the purpose of the provision is to make the law in question "apply consistently to reserved matters and otherwise".[29] In interpreting any provision of Scottish legislation, which could be read to be outside the competence of the Scottish Parliament, the courts are to read such a provision "as narrowly as is required for it to be within competence, if such a reading is possible".[30] Taken together, these provisions attempt to ensure that "if possible a construction should be given to the words which would avoid holding the legislation to be *ultra vires*" by requiring the courts to look at the "pith and substance" of the provision in question.[31]

Provisions of the Northern Ireland Assembly which could be read in a way as to be within the legislative competence of the Assembly, or in such a way as to be outside its competence are to be read in such a way as to be within competence.[32] This approach is consistent with making the devolved legislatures masters in their own house.

---

[28] Scotland Act, s.29(3).
[29] Scotland Act, s.29(4).
[30] Scotland Act, s.101(2).
[31] Per W. B. Maginess Q.C., Attorney-General for Northern Ireland in *Belfast Corpn v. OD Cars Ltd* [1960] AC 490, 503.
[32] Northern Ireland Act, s.83.

No amount of rules of construction can however resolve the problem that may arise where two legislatures are at loggerheads.[33] In this situation the obvious solution is amendment of the Scotland Act or the Northern Ireland Act to remove legislative competence from the devolved legislatures, a solution that brings with it obvious political consequences and dangers. In the absence of such amendment, the courts will have to deal with the problems of conflicting provisions.

This issue is one that has arisen in the context of membership of the European Union where it relates to the relationship between a validly enacted United Kingdom Act as against an equally valid rule of European law.[34] In these cases the rule in question derived its own validity within the legal order in which it was adopted and the question of a hierarchy only arose in the context of a clash between legal orders. The approach of the European Court has been to impose an obligation on the national judge to set aside the national law that conflicts with European law since in the hierarchy of legal orders European law prevails. It does so because the Members State of the European Union pooled their sovereignty to create a "new legal order of international law".[35]

It can be argued that devolution has created "a new legal order of constitutional law" within the United Kingdom. If this is the case, and if it is not then devolution is a waste of time and effort, then the kind of arguments used by the European Court in considering the relationships between legal orders could be adopted in determining how courts might approach the issue of the hierarchy of legal norms in a devolved United Kingdom. The European Court undoubtedly wished to secure the European settlement and its reasoning reflects this desire. The Court argued that it is necessary to examine the objectives underlying the European settlement. These were to create a new legal order and to endow the institutions created with a

---

[33] In the 1950s Sir Ivor Jennings had suggested that it would be unconstitutional for Westminster to legislate in an area devolved to Northern Ireland. His views are discussed in V. Bogdanor, *Devolution* (Oxford: OUP, 1979) at 50. Bogdanor states that Westminster's supremacy was more theoretical than real until "the normal working of devolution had been disrupted by sectarian violence".

[34] Case 26/62 *Van Gend en Loos v. Nederlandse Administratie der Belastingen* [1963] E.C.R. 105; case 6/64 *Costa v. ENEL* [1964] E.C.R. 585; case 11/70 *Internationale Handelsgesellschaft v. Einfuhr-und Vorratselle fur Getreide* [1970] E.C.R. 1125; case 106/77 *Amministrazione delle Finanze dello Stato v. Simmenthal* [1978] E.C.R. 629.

[35] Case 26/62 in note 34.

capacity to act independently of the States that created them. To ensure that this system operates effectively it is necessary for the judiciary to police the settlement to ensure that the rights of individuals are protected as a device to secure the system itself.

The same line of argument can be applied by analogy to the devolution settlement. The objectives of the "new legal order of constitutional law" in the United Kingdom are to modernise the United Kingdom constitution by decentralising power to bring government closer to the people and by transferring legislative competencies to newly created institutions. In areas covered by the legislation, Westminster has transferred its legislative powers to the parliaments in Scotland and Northern Ireland and, so long as they operate within their own spheres, the primary legislation adopted by them must be applied within the relevant region. In case of a conflict, the courts should apply the primary legislation of the devolved legislature. This does not give the courts a power to review the legality of United Kingdom legislation, merely to set it aside in case of conflict in order to ground the devolution settlement in objective principles based on the rule of law.

It may be that this approach is too radical for those who retain an adherence to a belief in the legislative supremacy of the United Kingdom Parliament and the sacrosanct nature of all Acts of that Parliament. They would argue that the legislation adopted by the United Kingdom Parliament has a superior characteristic to Acts of the devolved legislatures and that such legislation must be automatically applied by the courts. This approach, the purist approach, may maintain the integrity of the theory of the legislative supremacy of the United Kingdom Parliament but it ignores the political reality of the genuine transfer of power that has occurred under devolution.

Legislative competence

The Scottish Parliament and the Northern Ireland Assembly are, therefore, given powers to adopt primary legislation in the fullest sense of that term. Before examining the scope of this legislative competence, it is important to distinguish the terminology used in the Scotland Act and the Northern Ireland Act since the approach in the legislation is different and the terminology is confusing. Both Acts confer a general power to legislate. In the case of Scotland, this general power is limited in three ways. First, Schedule 4 lists those enactments that are protected from modification. The Scottish Parliament is restricted from modifying any of the measures listed in that Schedule.[36] Second, an Act of the Scottish Parliament is outwith its competence if it relates to reserved matters.[37] Reserved matters are listed in Schedule 5. Finally, the Scottish Parliament may not remove the Lord Advocate from his position as head of the system of criminal prosecution in Scotland.[38]

By contrast, the Northern Ireland Act distinguishes entrenched, excepted, reserved and transferred matters. Hadfield explains this distinction in terms of its basis in the earlier devolution legislation in force in Northern Ireland.[39] Entrenched matters are listed in section 7 of the Northern Ireland Act. These include most of the European Communities Act 1972, the Human Rights Act 1998 and several provisions of the Northern Ireland Act itself. The Northern Ireland Assembly has no power to modify these entrenched provisions. They are equivalent to provisions protected from modification in the Scottish legislation. A second limitation operates in respect of excepted matters. It is outside the legislative competence of the Northern Ireland Assembly to enact legislation that deals with an excepted matter.[40] Excepted matters are listed in Schedule 2. Thus reserved matters in the Scottish legislation is the broadly speaking functional equivalent of excepted matters in the Northern Ireland legislation. By contrast, reserved matters, under the Northern Ireland Act, are matters that are within the legislative competence of the Northern Ireland Assembly but the power to legislate is conditional upon the consent of the Secretary of State.[41] They are listed in Schedule 3. Transferred matters are all others. The Secretary of State can make an Order, subject to obtaining the consent of the Northern Ireland Assembly voting on a cross-community basis, to make reserved matters excepted and vice versa. This more complex scheme is intended to allow for the rolling out of additional devolved matters over time.

Despite the difference in terminology and the precise scope of the legislation the model of devolution in both the Scotland Act and the

---

[36] Scotland Act, s.29(2)(c).
[37] Scotland Act, s.29(2)(b).
[38] Scotland Act, s.29(2)(e).
[39] B. Hadfield, "The Nature of Devolution in Scotland and Northern Ireland: Key Issues of Responsibility and Control" (1999) 3 *Edinburgh Law Review* 3.
[40] Northern Ireland Act, s.6(1)(b).
[41] Northern Ireland Act, s.8(b).

Northern Ireland Act is the same. This model has been described as a retaining model whereby the United Kingdom Parliament devolves a general legislative power but retains certain defined functions for itself.[42] The legislation therefore details the areas in which the devolved legislatures do not have competence. The precedent for this approach is the Government of Ireland Act 1920 and it contrasts with the approach taken in the Scotland Act 1978. Under the 1978 Act, the powers to be transferred to the Scottish Parliament were enumerated. The result of this approach was really to require specification of both transferred and devolved matters resulting in extremely complex legislation. The approach was criticised at the time of the 1978 Act as being inflexible so that "even the most minor allocation of functions will require legislation at Westminster, and the battles over devolution could be fought again and again with tedious regularity".[43]

Both the 1998 Acts transfer the power to legislate but limit this transfer by enumerating exceptions. Thus the Scottish Parliament can legislate on any matter provided that the matter is not one that is protected from modification under Schedule 4 or is a reserved matter and is listed in Schedule 5. The Northern Ireland Assembly may legislate on any transferred matter but it may not legislate to modify any entrenched matter nor may it legislate on any excepted matter. It may legislate on reserved matters with the consent of the Secretary of State.

Additional restrictions are placed on both the Scottish Parliament and the Northern Ireland Assembly.[44] Neither body can:

- legislate with extra-territorial effect
- pass legislation contrary to Community law
- pass legislation conflicting with a right provided by the European Convention on Human Rights.

In Northern Ireland legislation is also prohibited where it discriminates against any person or class on the grounds of religious belief or political opinion. This is one of the safeguards designed to protect both communities in Northern Ireland and to provide for parity of

---

[42] A. Page et al. n. 23, 46.
[43] V. Bogdanor, Devolution (Oxford: OUP, 1979) at 169.
[44] Scotland Act, s.29(2) and Northern Ireland Act, s.6(2).

esteem. No similar rule applies to the Scottish Parliament but, if current proposals for European Union legislation to outlaw discrimination are adopted, the Scottish Parliament will be bound by a Community obligation (as will the Westminster Parliament) not to introduce legislation that discriminates on the grounds of religious or political belief.[45]

Unless the legislation provides that it is outwith the legislative competence of either the Scottish Parliament or the Northern Ireland Assembly either legislature is free to enact legislation on any matter. Having said that, it is not always an easy matter to determine the exact scope of the legislative competence of one of the devolved legislatures. For example, under the Scotland Act, the subject matter of the Sex Discrimination Act 1975 is reserved but there are exceptions to this reservation. The Scottish Parliament may encourage equal opportunities and in particular the observance of equal opportunities requirements.[46] The question has arisen as to what type of obligation can be imposed on Scottish local authorities by the Scottish Parliament to encourage equal opportunities in Scottish schools.[47] In the context of the debate on the Standards in Scotland's Schools, etc., Bill, the question was raised whether local authorities could be required to include an account of the way in which they will ensure equal opportunities in Scottish schools. The debate then turned in the meaning to be given to the exceptions in Schedule 5. Malcolm Chisholm MSP expressed his uncertainty over the meaning to be given to Schedule 5. He said "my worry is that there is some uncertainty even—dare I say it—among the law officers and that this may be a moving target".

This type of issue will inevitably arise in many different contexts so that the exact scope of devolution will only become apparent over time. It must be acknowledged that the borderline is fluid or, as Chisholm states, a moving target. Whichever model of devolution had been chosen, similar problems were always likely to emerge. The boundary between reserved or excepted matters and devolved matters will therefore become clarified over time.

---

[45] The Commission published proposals for new legislation at the end of 1999 with the intention of adopting two anti-discrimination measures by the end of 2000. The first measure outlaws discrimination on the ground of race, the second deals with discrimination on the grounds of racial or ethnic origin, religion or belief, disability, age or sexual orientation.

[46] Scotland Act, Schedule 5 L2.

[47] Equal Opportunities Committee Official Report, meeting 12, May 22, 2000, cols 678–686.

Legislative procedures

Both the Scottish Parliament and the Northern Ireland Assembly are unicameral. In exercising legislative powers both must, therefore, ensure adequate scrutiny of the provisions of a Bill to ensure that the legislation is suitable to achieve the purposes set out in the Bill and to ensure that it falls within the legislative competence of the Parliament/Assembly. In addition, in Scotland, the Consultative Steering Group (CSG), in making their recommendations on legislative procedures, was concerned to make the legislative procedures as participative and as open as possible. For this reason the CSG recommended that there should be a recognisable pre-legislative stage in which consultation should take place with relevant bodies or interested parties and that there should be a duty on the Executive to explain in full to the Parliament the policy goals and the anticipated consequences of a particular Bill.[48] This approach has been accepted and formalised in Standing Orders. In Northern Ireland, participation on cultural, economic and social matters is encouraged through the statutory Civic Forum.[49]

(1) PRE-LEGISLATIVE SCRUTINY

It was anticipated that most Scottish legislation would be initiated by a member of the Scottish Executive. In the first year of the life of the Scottish Parliament five Acts have been passed, all five originating as Executive Bills. However, of the 12 Bills in progress, five are Members Bills and seven are Executive Bills. The importance of Members Bills should not therefore be ignored. The proposal for an Executive Bill is normally intimated in the statement made by the First Minister to the Parliament at the beginning of a session in which he/she sets out the Executive's policy objectives and legislative programme. Any Bill introduced by a member of the Executive must be accompanied by five documents:

- a written statement from the member of the Scottish Executive in charge of the Bill to the effect that the provisions of the Bill,

---

[48] The Consultative Steering Group on the Scottish Parliament, *Shaping Scotland's Parliament* (Edinburgh: The Scottish Office, 1998) at 42–56.
[49] Northern Ireland Act, s.56 requires consultation on social economic and cultural matters.

in his/her view, falls within the legislative competence of the Parliament[50]

- a written statement from the Presiding Officer setting out his/her view as to whether the provisions of the Bill are within the legislative competence of the Parliament[51]

- a Financial Memorandum setting out estimates of administrative and compliance costs distinguishing costs falling on the Scottish Administration, local authorities and other bodies, individuals and businesses[52]

- an Explanatory Note summarising what the Bill does

- a Policy Memorandum providing information on the policy objectives of the Bill, any alternative approaches that were considered, the consultation that was undertaken and the results of that consultation, an assessment of the effects of the legislation in terms of equal opportunities, human rights, islands communities, sustainable development and other relevant matters.

These pre-legislative procedures are designed to fulfil several functions. The most important function is to ensure that the Parliament legislates only in those areas that have been devolved under the Scotland Act, thereby avoiding potential future challenges to Acts of the Scottish Parliament in the courts. Pre-legislative checks, provided that they are carried out scrupulously, should be able to avert such challenges. In addition, they are intended to ensure that consultation is normally carried out at an early stage of proposed legislation. The requirement to publish the accompanying documents is intended to provide for a more open legislative procedure in which information is provided at the earliest stage, thereby giving interested parties an opportunity to comment and perhaps influence the style and shape of the legislation.

Somewhat similar pre-legislative stages are required in Northern Ireland. Both the relevant Minister[53] and the Presiding Officer[54] must

---

[50] This is a statutory requirement, see Scotland Act, s.31(1).

[51] This is a statutory requirement, see Scotland Act, s.31(2).

[52] This and the following two requirements are found in Standing Orders of the Scottish Parliament Rule 9.3. The initial standing orders of the Scottish Parliament were provided in S.I. 1999/1095 The Scotland Act (Transitory and Transitional Provisions) (Standing Orders and Parliamentary Publications) Order. These have been superseded by Standing Orders Edition 2. They were made by the Resolution of the Scottish Parliament of December 9, and came into force on December 17, 1999.

[53] Northern Ireland Act, s.9.

[54] Northern Ireland Act, s.10(1).

provide a written statement that the proposed Bill is within the legislative competence of the Northern Ireland Assembly. In addition the Presiding Officer must also refer a Bill to the Secretary of State where a provision of a Bill deals with an excepted matter and is ancillary to provisions dealing with reserved or transferred matters or it deals with a transferred matter. In these cases, the Secretary of State must indicate his/her consent to the matter being dealt with in the Bill unless he/she indicates that the Bill is, in fact, within the legislative competence of the Assembly.[55] These additional provisions are necessary because of the distinction between reserved and excepted matters outlined above. Because of the more limited nature of the transfer of powers to the Northern Ireland Assembly there is likely to be a much greater overlap between the functions of Westminster and Belfast. The Secretary of State is therefore given a more instrumental role in the early stages of the legislative procedures.

(2) PARLIAMENTARY STAGES

Both the Scotland Act and the Northern Ireland Act require that the standing orders of the devolved legislatures provide for three stages in the enactment of legislation.[56] There must be a general debate on the Bill with the opportunity for members to vote on the general principles of the legislation. The second stage is the opportunity for detailed consideration of the provisions of a Bill, followed by the opportunity to vote and a third and final stage at which a Bill can be passed or rejected. Standing orders of the Scottish Parliament require all three stages to be completed in one parliamentary session.[57] Failing completion in this time scale a new Bill in similar terms may be introduced at the next session. There must be at least two weeks between the completion of stage 1 and the beginning of stage 2 and, if the Bill is amended at stage 2, a further gap of two weeks is required between stage 2 and stage 3. This is to allow MSPs to reconsider the provisions of the Bill in the light of amendments. If a Bill is rejected it falls and cannot be reintroduced within six months.

---

[55] Northern Ireland Act, s.10(2).
[56] Scotland Act, s.36, Northern Ireland Act, s.13.
[57] This section examines in more detail the procedures adopted by the Scottish Parliament since there is very limited experience from the Northern Ireland Assembly upon which to draw.

In the first two stages the role of the committee is paramount both in terms of scrutiny and amendment.

Stage 1. On introduction of the Bill into the Scottish Parliament, the Parliamentary Bureau refers it to a lead committee within whose remit the Bill falls.[58] The function of the committee is to consider and report on the general principles of the Bill. Other committees may also consider the Bill and report on its general principles. If a Bill contains a power to make subordinate legislation, the Parliamentary Bureau also refers the Bill to the Subordinate Legislation Committee for is consideration of those provisions. The lead committee must report on the Bill taking into consideration the views of any other committee that has been involved in discussing the Bill. Parliament then considers the general principles of the Bill in the light of the lead committee's report and decides whether those principles are agreed to. If the Parliament as a whole agrees to the principles of the Bill it proceeds to stage 2. Alternatively, the Bill may be remitted back to the lead committee for further consideration at this stage. Without the agreement of Parliament on the general principles the Bill falls.

Stage 2 is the detailed scrutiny of the sections and schedules of the Bill. This scrutiny can be conducted either by the lead committee or by a Committee of the Whole Parliament. The Parliamentary Bureau is responsible for deciding which of these two procedures to follow. Bills can be amended at this stage. Amendments can be proposed by any MSP after the completion of stage one. Such an MSP may attend the committee to explain the amendment but may not vote. The Member of the Executive proposing the Bill, if he/she is not a member of the committee, may also attend but may not vote. It is anticipated that this second stage will be the most important stage in the parliamentary procedure since the committee structure of the Parliament is designed to allow individual MSPs to develop expertise in the field covered by their committees. In addition committees may, with the consent of the Parliamentary Bureau, appoint advisers to conduct inquiries or to advise the committee on particular matters. The level of expertise amongst MSPs can thus be augmented in the committee if this is necessary.

---

[58] Subject committees are discussed in Chapter 2 above.

Stage 3. The Bill, as amended where appropriate, then passes to the third stage. This stage is taken at a meeting of the Parliament and involves a decision on the question of whether the Bill should be passed. Amendments are possible at this stage and there is also the possibility to remit parts of the Bill back to the lead committee for further consideration. A quorum of one quarter of the members is necessary for a valid vote on any Bill to take place. A Bill may be reconsidered after it has been passed if a question on its *vires* has been referred to the Judicial Committee of the Privy Council or if a reference has been made to the European Court of Justice.

Additional safeguards relating to equality and human rights issues are built into the legislative procedures under the Northern Ireland Act. The first safeguard originates in the Belfast Agreement. Strand One of the Agreement states that the Assembly may appoint a special Committee to "examine and report on whether a proposal for legislation is in conformity with equality requirements, including the EHCR/Bill of Rights".[59] The Committee thus established was intended to have the "power to call people and papers" to assist the Assembly in its consideration of the matter. The Assembly was then to continue the report of the Committee to determine the matter in accordance with the cross community consent procedure. This aspect of the Belfast Agreement was translated into section 13(3)(a) of the Northern Ireland Act which provides that standing orders may require scrutiny of a Bill by a committee of the Assembly established for this purpose. Such scrutiny can be required by a member of the Executive or by a subject committee. This provision is necessary because of the restriction of the legislative competence of the Northern Ireland Assembly discussed above in relation to non-discrimination on religious or political grounds.

A second safeguard is also found in the legislation. Section 13(4)(a) provides that standing orders must require that the Presiding Officer send a copy of each Bill, as soon as reasonably practicable after introduction, to the Northern Ireland Human Rights Commission to establish its compatibility with human rights standards.[60]

A final safeguard to protect human rights against any possible infringement by the Northern Ireland Assembly rests with the

---

[59] *The Agreement Reached in Multi-party Negotiations* CM 4292 (1998).
[60] Northern Ireland Act, ss.68–70 establish the Northern Ireland Human Rights Commission. On the work of the Commission see B. Dickson, "New Human Rights Protections in Northern Ireland" (1999) 24 E.L.Rev. HR/3.

Presiding Officer. Before the Assembly enters its final stage, the Presiding Officer must again scrutinise a Bill to assure him/herself that it is still within the legislative competence of the Northern Ireland Assembly after any amendments have been made.[61]

Thus stringent safeguards have been put in place in Northern Ireland to ensure that the Assembly does not infringe the equality provisions of the Belfast Agreement. The Belfast Agreement had committed all parties to the mutual respect, the civil rights and the religious liberties of everyone in Northern Ireland. This commitment was against the background of communal conflict. Without that background the scrutiny rules would seem overly prescriptive and excessively mistrustful of the way in which the Assembly will use its powers. The Scottish Parliament, by contrast, is not subject to such rigorous scrutiny. The procedures are intended to reassure the nationalist community in the light of past practice at Stormont. They do however protect the interests of the community as a whole.

(3) Post legislative scrutiny

After completion of the parliamentary stages in Scotland, the Advocate General, the Lord Advocate or the Attorney General may, within four weeks, submit a question as to the legislative competence of the Parliament to pass any provision of the Bill to the Judicial Committee of the Privy Council.[62] In the same four weeks period the Secretary of State may make an Order prohibiting the Presiding Officer from submitting a Bill for Royal Assent if he/she believes that its provisions are incompatible with any international obligation or would raise issues of national security or defence or if it would adversely affect the law as it applies to reserved matters.[63] In the absence of such a reference or Order, the Presiding Officer may then submit the Bill for Royal Assent.

In Northern Ireland, the Attorney General for Northern Ireland may make a reference on the question of competence to the Judicial Committee within a four week period of the Bill being passed.[64] In the absence of any such legal challenge, it is the Secretary of State who then submits the Bill for Royal Assent.

---

[61] Northern Ireland Act, s.10.
[62] Scotland Act, s.33.
[63] Scotland Act, s.35.
[64] Northern Ireland Act, s.11.

In comparing the provisions of the Scotland Act and the Northern Ireland Act it can be seen that there are key differences in the procedural rules. Broadly speaking, it can be seen that the Scottish Parliament acts under fewer constraints than the Northern Ireland Assembly. First, the Secretary of State for Scotland has a residual role in the adoption of legislation as compared to the Secretary of State for Northern Ireland. This can be explained by the difference in the approach taken in the legislation. In particular, it is necessary because of the inclusion of the distinct category of reserved matters in the Northern Ireland legislation whereby the Secretary of State is required to give his/her consent before the Northern Ireland Assembly can enact legislation on these matters. This is a historic legacy and can be explained by the fact that the Northern Ireland Act follows the pattern of earlier devolution legislation. The Scottish legislation does not draw on this earlier tradition.

Absent from the Northern Ireland legislation is a role for a Northern Ireland law officer. The Attorney General for Northern Ireland is a United Kingdom government minister. There is no equivalent to Scotland's Lord Advocate in the Northern Ireland legal system and no new post has been created under the Northern Ireland Act.[65] Thus references to the Judicial Committee, where necessary, must always be made by a members of the United Kingdom government rather than having a role for a law officer of the devolved executive. The more central role given to the Secretary of State for Northern Ireland and the Attorney General suggests a closer link, perhaps even a greater degree of control, between the United Kingdom government and the Northern Ireland Assembly than exists between the United Kingdom government and the Scottish Parliament.

The Northern Ireland Assembly is subject to greater procedural safeguards as regards protection of human rights and equality provisions. Again this feature is explicable in historical terms and in the insistence of nationalist negotiators to the Belfast Agreement to write in safeguards into the legislation. One of the key demands of the nationalist negotiators was the inclusion of an equality and human rights agenda for the new institutions of government in Northern Ireland.

---

[65] For a discussion of the role and functions of the Law Officers see Chapter 6 below.

(4) Types of Bills (Scotland only)

The devolution legislation does not make any distinction between government Bills and private members Bills. These distinctions are drawn in standing orders. The standing orders of the Scottish Parliament distinguish several different types of Bills; Executive Bills, Members Bills, Consolidation Bills, Budget Bills, Private Bills, Consolidation Bills, Statute Law Repeal Bills, Statute Law Reform Bills and Emergency Bills. Each of these Bills follows a slightly different procedure to that outlined above.

1. Members Bills. Any MSP may initiate up to two Bills per year. Members' Bills are defined in Standing Orders as being "a Public Bill other than a Committee Bill introduced by a member who is not a member of the Scottish Executive . . . its purpose is to give effect to a proposal for a Bill made by that member". The name of the MSP proposing the Bill, its short title and a note explaining the purpose of the Bill are lodged with the Clerk who then publishes these details. Other MSPs may then intimate their support. A Bill must attract the support of 11 other MSPs before it can proceed further otherwise it falls and it cannot be re-introduced within six months. Having passed this hurdle a Bill must then go through the stages outlined above except that there is no requirement on the part of an individual MSP to provide a statement as to the legislative competence of the Parliament nor need he/she provide a Policy Memorandum. The Presiding Officer must, however, take a view on the legislative competence issue and make his/her views known.

In the first year of the Scottish Parliament five Members Bills have been introduced and parliamentary time has been made available to debate them. In many ways the most interesting of these Bills is the Abolition of Poindings and Warrant Sales Bill introduced by Tommy Sheridan MSP who is the only member of the Scottish Socialist Party in the Scottish Parliament. His success in bringing legislation forward with the support of back bench Labour MSPs has been seen as a precedent for the importance of individual MSPs and as an example of the new politics in which Parliament is restored. A legal challenge was mounted against Lord Watson MSP in his attempt to introduce the Protection of Wild Mammals (Scotland) Bill into the Scottish Parliament.[66] The

---

[66] *Whaley v. Lord Watson of Invergowrie* [2000] SLT 475.

case brought against Lord Watson demonstrates the need for individual MSPs to have support in preparing and drafting proposed legislation but also the requirement to declare such support in the Register of Members' Interests.

2. Committee Bills. A committee of the Parliament may introduce a Bill on a matter that falls within the committee's remit. The committee may hold an inquiry to determine the need for legislation and the kind of legislation required. The Parliamentary Bureau may also direct a proposal for legislation from any MSP to the relevant committee to consider whether the committee should take up the issue. A proposal for a Committee Bill must be accompanied by a report setting out the committee's recommendations as to the provisions to be included in the Bill and may also include a draft of the Bill itself. If Parliament agrees on the need for legislation, the committee convener may either instruct the drafting of the Bill or introduce the Bill into the Parliament where a draft has already been prepared unless a Scottish Minister indicates that he/she will take over and introduce an Executive Bill. At Stage I, the general principles are not considered by the lead committee and the procedure immediately moves to a consideration of the principles of the Bill by the whole Parliament. Again the Bill must be accompanied by a statement of the Presiding Officer on its *vires* and a Financial Memorandum.

The CSG had believed that Committee Bills might have become an important feature of the work of the Scottish Parliament. To date there is little evidence to show that this will be the case as no Committee Bills have been introduced.

3. Budget Bills are a special type of Executive Bill. They may only be introduced by a member of the Scottish Executive and their function is to authorise sums to be paid out of the Scottish Consolidated Fund or to authorise payments of sums received. They may also amend Budget Acts. Budget Bills do not require an accompanying Financial Memorandum, an Explanatory Note or a Policy Memorandum. At stage 1 the Bill goes immediately to the Parliament rather than to a committee for the consideration of the principles of the Bill and stage 2 must be taken by the Finance Committee. There is no requirement for the two weeks gap between stage 1 and 2 as is required with other Bills. Stage 3 must begin within 20 days of the Bill being introduced into Parliament and if all stages are not completed by the end of 30 days after the Bill's introduction then the Bill fails. Amendments to Budget Bills can only be moved by a member of the Scottish Executive. If

the Bill is dependent on a Resolution of the Parliament to vary the rate of income tax and that Resolution is defeated then the Bill also fails. If a Budget Bill fails for any reason a new Bill can be introduced immediately.

4. Private Bills can be introduced by an individual person, a body corporate or an unincorporated association of persons (promoter) for the purpose of obtaining for the promoter particular powers or benefits in excess of or in conflict with the general law. They can be introduced only on March 27 or November 27, or the next sitting day after these dates if there is no sitting on the set dates. They must be signed by the promoter. At stage 1 the lead committee must report on the need for the provision sought and any opposition to it. The committee may require the promoter to obtain additional information or to publicise the need for the legislation. At stage 2 the committee may authorise a reporter or an expert to conduct an inquiry on the need for and the suitability of the Bill.

5. Consolidation Bills are used to restate the existing law or, if need be, to give effect to recommendations of the Law Commissions. Where appropriate, they may be known as Codification Bills. Consolidation Bills do not require accompanying documents but they must include tables of derivations and destinations. The Parliamentary Bureau establishes a Consolidation Committee to act as lead committee bearing in mind the need for expertise in the membership of the committee. At stage 1 the Consolidation Committee reports on whether the law should be restated. Parliament votes on the report without debate. During stage 2 no amendments are permitted that would change the character of the provisions of the Bill. At stage 3 Parliament decides the matter without debate. Amendments are possible at this stage only if they are necessary to give effect to the recommendations of the Law Commission for Scotland.

6. Statute Law Repeal Bills are used to repeal spent enactments in accordance with recommendations of the Law Commission. The procedure is the same as for Consolidation Bills except that the Parliamentary Bureau will establish a Statute Law Repeals Committee to consider the Bill.

7. Statute Law Revision Bills are used to revise statutes by repealing enactments no longer in force or have become unnecessary. They may also re-enact provisions of legislation of either the United Kingdom or the Scottish Parliament

which are otherwise spent. Here the lead committee is to be known as the Statute Law Revision Committee.

8. Emergency Bills. Any member of the Scottish Executive or any Scottish junior minister may propose that an Executive Bill be treated as an Emergency Bill. If Parliament agrees expedited procedures can be used to get the Bill through Parliament in a single day. At stage 1 the Bill is referred immediately to Parliament for a decision on its principles, a committee report is not required. Stage 2 is taken by a Committee of the Whole Parliament and there is no requirement that there should be a two weeks gap between stages 1 and 2.

The very first Act of the Scottish Parliament was adopted following the emergency procedure. The Mental Health (Public Safety and Appeals) (Scotland) Act 1999 has been challenged in the courts as being contrary to a Convention right and therefore outside the legislative competence of the Scottish Parliament.[67] This case perhaps proves, if poof were necessary, that the emergency procedure does not provide sufficient time and opportunity to discuss complex matters of *vires* that arise out of the need to ensure that Scottish legislation does not offend any Convention right. It is difficult to see how all these matters could be adequately dealt with in one single day.

The Role of the National Assembly for Wales in the adoption of Welsh primary legislation

Up until this point in the chapter there has been no discussion of the National Assembly for Wales. The National Assembly Advisory Group (NAAG) concluded that "the Assembly will not be a Parliament in the recognised sense of the term".[68] The National Assembly for Wales is a different kind of body than the Scottish Parliament or the Northern Ireland Assembly. The most significant difference is that the National Assembly for Wales does not have power to enact primary legislation. Whereas the Scotland Act and the Northern

---

[67] *Anderson, Doherty and Reid v. The Scottish Ministers and the Advocate General for Scotland*, reported on the Scottish Courts web site http://www.scotcourts.gov.uk/indexl.htm.
[68] National Assembly Advisory Group, *Consultation Document: National Assembly for Wales, have your say in how it will work* para. 3.6.

Ireland Act provide for legislative devolution, the Government of Wales Act provides for executive or administrative devolution. This means that the Assembly takes over most of the functions previously exercised in Wales by ministers in the Welsh office and by Ministers of the Crown in so far as their functions were relevant to Wales. Primary legislation will continue to be made in Westminster. One of the implications of this is that the Assembly requires to be brought into the Westminster legislative processes and this is done by making the Assembly an advisory body to the Westminster parliament on legislation in so far as that legislation affects Wales.

The White Paper on the National Assembly for Wales stated that "the Assembly will help to create the body of law which governs Wales".[69] Its own law making powers were to be restricted to the enactment of secondary legislation. However the White Paper went on to say that "the Bill will place a duty on the Secretary of State to consult the Assembly about the Government's programme for legislation after it has been announced in the Queen's speech." The Government of Wales Act does not, in fact, place a duty to consult on the Secretary of State. Instead it provides that he/she "shall undertake such consultation about the government's legislative programme for the session as appears to him to be appropriate". This consultation shall "include attending and participating in proceedings of the Assembly".[70] The Government of Wales Act gives to the Secretary of State therefore a discretion to decide on what aspects of the government's legislative programme he/she determines is appropriate for the purposes of consulting the National Assembly for Wales. It also gives a right to a United Kingdom government Minister to participate in proceedings of the National Assembly for Wales on at least one occasion despite the fact that he/she may not be a Member of the Assembly. This approach in the legislation suggests an agenda setting role for the Secretary of State but it is tempered by the right given to the National Assembly for Wales "to consider, and make appropriate representations about, any matter affecting Wales".[71] Thus the Assembly can seek to influence the government's legislative programme through this route if the Secretary of State should deem debate on any proposed legislation inappropriate.

These provisions have now been fleshed out by practice within the National Assembly for Wales. A Protocol was adopted in January

---

[69] *National Assembly for Wales,* Cm 3718 (1997).
[70] Government of Wales Act, s.31(1).
[71] Government of Wales Act, s.33.

2000 between the Assembly and the Secretary of State for Wales.[72] It recognises that the Secretary of State has three duties in relation to the passing of primary legislation covering Wales. He/she must consult the Assembly on the Government's legislative programme, he/she must ensure that Welsh interests are considered during the development and drafting of such legislation and he/she must steer the legislation through Parliament. As far as the Assembly is concerned, the Protocol interprets section 33 of the Government of Wales Act (the right to make appropriate representations) to include the right to propose Bills or amendments to Bills at any time. Given that Bills are drafted by Parliamentary Counsel, the Protocol states that there is no need for the National Assembly for Wales to provide a detailed draft of any proposed Bill. Instead, the motion should set out the "purpose and effect of the Bill in sufficient detail to enable the precise provisions to be drafted". In order to dovetail with the Government's legislative time-table, the Assembly agrees normally to submit its proposals for Bills during the first session in each calendar year for consideration by the Secretary of State. He/she in turn will bring any such proposals to the attention of the United Kingdom Cabinet Committee on the Queen's Speech and Future Legislation. The Secretary of State will liaise between this Committee and the National Assembly for Wales to ensure a free flow of information. The Protocol underlines the fact that there can be no guarantee that the Government will necessarily adopt a proposal from the National Assembly for Wales as part of its legislative programme since it retains the ultimate right to determine what is or is not included in such a programme. Considerations of Parliamentary time and the Government's own priorities must be considered alongside any requests for new Welsh legislation.

Where proposals for Bills are brought forward, the relevant subject committee of the Assembly will be involved in developing proposals. Subject committees will also be instrumental in proposing amendments—perhaps even to the extent of drafting such amendments. The relevant Assembly Secretary, who is automatically a member of the subject committee, will inform the Secretary of State of any such amendments.

These arrangements rely on goodwill on the part of the National Assembly for Wales in its dealings with the Secretary of State and in

---

[72] The initiative for the protocol came from the Assembly Cabinet. See *Devolution—A Dynamic, Settled Process* (Cardiff; Institute for Welsh Affairs).

return require a commitment on the part of the latter to transmit Assembly policies to the United Kingdom Cabinet. There are clear benefits for the Secretary of State if he/she develops close working relationships with the Assembly. First, the National Assembly for Wales is the voice of Wales. Having the support of the Assembly strengthens the hand of the Secretary of State in his/her dealings with Cabinet colleagues. On a more practical level, the Assembly could provide logistical support to an Office whose ability to "participate effectively across such a wide range of activity in the Whitehall and Westminster processes" has been questioned.[73]

In comparing the role of the National Assembly for Wales in the adoption of primary legislation for Wales with the fully fledged legislative powers transferred to the Scottish Parliament and the Northern Ireland Assembly, it is difficult to escape the conclusion that the National Assembly for Wales is very much the lesser or weaker party. Under these arrangements there will never be any guarantee that specifically Welsh priorities will be taken on board by the United Kingdom Government. It may be argued that in the past, because of the integration of the English and Welsh legal systems, separate legislation was rarely required and that this situation has been continued. However, the Government has stated that "to do things differently in different parts of the United Kingdom is not an accidental consequence of devolution; it was our express intention".[74] If the National Assembly for Wales wants to do things differently, however, it will have to rely on the United Kingdom Parliament to provide the means for it to do so.

Scrutiny of the Administration

The principle of responsible or accountable government is a key element of United Kingdom constitutional law. The duty on members of the Government to account to Parliament for their activities and for the efficient running of their departments is a well understood concept. The scrutiny of the administration is therefore considered to be one of the key functions of the United Kingdom Parliament.[75] This part of the chapter examines the mechanisms that

---

[73] J. Osmond, *Devolution Relaunched* (Cardiff; Institute for Welsh Affairs, 2000) at 40.
[74] HL Deb vol 612 col. 6 April 10, 2000.
[75] See, for example, A. W. Bradley and K. D. Ewing, *Constitutional and Administrative Law* (12th ed.) (Harlow: Longman, 1997) at 225.

can be used by the elected institutions to bring the executive to account.

In treating this issue it is necessary to distinguish the arrangements for Scotland and Northern Ireland from the arrangements for Wales. As is apparent from the first part of this chapter the form of devolution chosen for Scotland and Northern Ireland is different from that chosen for Wales. In Scotland and Northern Ireland legislative devolution has resulted in a transfer of powers from the United Kingdom Parliament to the devolved legislatures. No similar transfer has been made to the National Assembly for Wales where the form of devolution is characterised as executive or administrative devolution. The United Kingdom Parliament has not transferred any of its powers to the National Assembly for Wales but has transferred executive powers from Ministers of the Crown to the Assembly. The National Assembly for Wales is itself the executive. The consequences of this difference in the form of devolution become apparent in examining the scrutiny function.

Accountability—the Welsh Model

The particular structure of the National Assembly for Wales raises some difficulties in discussing the accountability of the executive in traditional terms. The relationship between the Assembly Cabinet[76] and the Welsh Assembly is not comparable to that between the United Kingdom Cabinet and the United Kingdom Parliament or to that of the Scottish Cabinet to the Scottish Parliament. Under the Welsh devolution settlement there has been a transfer to the Assembly of ministerial functions. Legislative functions are not transferred to the Assembly and ministerial functions are not transferred to Welsh ministers. It is the Assembly which is to exercise functions previously exercised by Ministers of the Crown. The Assembly then delegates the implementation of these functions to the First Secretary and Secretaries appointed by him/her. The Welsh Cabinet exercises its functions therefore on behalf of the Assembly and in co-operation with it. This means that the other members of the Assembly are entitled to question the members of the Assembly Cabinet but they are also entitled to participate, by way of the

---

[76] For a discussion of the Assembly Cabinet see Chapter 4 below.

committee structure, in the development of policy. This is the reason why the NAAG called the system established under the Government of Wales Act a modified cabinet system since there is no clear division of functions between the executive and the legislative arms of government. All AMs are members of the executive arm of government in Wales since the Assembly collectively exercises functions delegated from Ministers of the Crown and all the Assembly Secretaries are equally part of the legislative arm in so far as the Assembly has the power to adopt subordinate legislation.

Accountability in these circumstances takes on a slightly different meaning to that used in traditional constitutional law and theory in the United Kingdom. As discussed in Chapter 4, the First Secretary is elected by the Assembly.[77] He/she may thereafter make a certain number of appointments to the post of Assembly Secretary.[78] The Assembly First Secretary and the Assembly Secretaries together form the Assembly Cabinet.[79] The First Secretary must allocate accountability in the fields in which the Assembly has functions to one of the Assembly Secretaries or retain accountability for himself/herself.[80] The Government of Wales Act defines accountability in terms of a linkage between a member of the executive committee and a field. Accountability therefore means that the Assembly Secretary "is the member of the executive committee accountable to the Assembly . . . for the exercise of the Assembly's functions in that field".[81] The mechanism whereby accountability is to be ensured is the use of oral or written questions. The Government of Wales Act requires standing orders to make provision to allow each AM to question "each member of the executive committee about the exercise of the Assembly's functions about the field or fields in which he is accountable".[82] Accountability under this model therefore means control over delegated powers. The National Assembly for Wales delegates its functions to members of the Assembly Cabinet who must answer to the Assembly for the exercise of those functions.

After the First Secretary has allocated accountability to an Assembly Secretary, the Assembly is required to set up a subject committee

---

[77] Government of Wales Act, s.53(1).
[78] Government of Wales Act, s.53(2).
[79] Government of Wales Act, s.56.
[80] Government of Wales Act, s.56(3).
[81] Government of Wales Act, s.56(5).
[82] Government of Wales Act, s.56(7)(a).

which exactly parallels the responsibilities of the Assembly Secretary.[83] The Assembly Secretary becomes a member of that committee but cannot chair it.[84] As discussed in Chapter 2, one of the functions of the subject committees is to contribute to the development of policies. In a sense this committee structure provides a form of collegiate government and collective policy and decision making. The Assembly Secretary must participate in the work of the subject committee and provide information on the policy of the Assembly Cabinet to enable the committee to reach informed decisions. However he/she is not accountable to the committee but is part of it. Accountability is always owed to the National Assembly for Wales as a whole since it is the Assembly that has delegated its functions.

Issues relating to individual responsibility have arisen in the operation of the National Assembly for Wales. The First Secretary and the Assembly Secretaries are accountable to the Assembly for the powers delegated to them. The Assembly elects the First Secretary who then chooses his/her Cabinet team. To continue to exercise delegated powers, members of the Assembly Cabinet including the First Secretary must command sufficient support of the Assembly to get their business through. The Government of Wales Act is silent on the effect of a vote of no confidence. When Christine Gwyther, the Secretary responsible for agriculture, lost a motion of no confidence, she did not resign her post since she had the support of the then First Secretary, Alun Michael. However, in his turn Alun Michael lost a vote of no confidence in the Assembly in February 2000. The particular cause of concern was in relation to E.U. structural funding. Assembly Members wanted some form of guarantee that the United Kingdom government would match E.U. funding in Wales under the principle of additionality. AMs were not convinced that Alun Michael could guarantee this. A motion of no confidence in the First Secretary was tabled in February 2000. The First Secretary indicated that he would stand for re-election if the vote were lost. However, hours before the vote was due, he resigned as First Secretary. The Assembly proceeded to the vote and the motion of no confidence was passed by 31 votes to 27 with one abstention. If Alun Michael had not resigned, Plaid Cymru had indicated that it would vote to revoke all powers delegated to the First Secretary and other Assembly Secretaries.[85]

---

[83] Government of Wales Act, s.57.
[84] Government of Wales Act, s.57(4).
[85] The story of the no confidence vote is told in J. Osmond (ed.) *Devolution Relaunched* (Cardiff: Institute for Welsh Affairs, 2000).

Individual ministerial responsibility in the Welsh context ultimately turns on the ultimate sanction of revocation of the delegation of powers to the First Secretary or any other Assembly Secretary. This sanction is, of course, more readily available where the Assembly Cabinet is attempting to run as a minority government. Then the threat of a vote of no confidence is a powerful weapon. The consequences of such a vote are interesting. The National Assembly for Wales, unlike the Westminster Parliament, is elected for a fixed term. A vote of no confidence in the Prime Minister or the United Kingdom government would normally lead to dissolution of Parliament and a new election. This option was not open to Alun Michael nor was it open to the Assembly as a whole. Following a vote of no confidence, therefore, the Assembly has to agree on the person or persons who replaces the First Secretary or the Assembly Secretaries and these individuals must then work towards retaining the support of the Assembly. In this context, concepts of individual ministerial responsibility or accountability are central to the operation of the Assembly.

Accountability—the Northern Irish Model

The relationship between the Northern Ireland Executive and the Northern Ireland Assembly is extremely complex. All of the institutional arrangements are based on principles of cross community support. Thus there is no single person who is head of government in Northern Ireland. Instead a bicephalous head of government, "the First Minister and Deputy First Minister" head up a multi-party Executive chosen on the basis of the d'Hondt formula.[86] Just as the electoral arrangements provide for proportional representation to ensure an adequate representation of the two communities in Northern Ireland so too do the arrangements for the choice of Executive ensure that both communities are represented in government.

It is a condition of office that all Ministers, including the First Minister and the Deputy First Minister, affirm a pledge of office whose terms were agreed in the multi-party negotiations leading to the Good Friday Agreement.[87] The Northern Ireland Act requires the

---

[86] See Chapter 4 below for a fuller explanation of the Northern Ireland Executive.
[87] *The Agreement Reached in Multi-party Negotiations* CM 4292 (1998).

First Minister and the Deputy First Minister,[88] all Ministers[89] and all Junior Ministers[90] to affirm the Pledge of Office whose text is found in Schedule 4 of the Act. The most important provisions of that pledge in terms of accountability to the Northern Ireland Assembly are those that commit the Minister to non-violence and peaceful and democratic means of government and to serve all the people of Northern Ireland equally. The task of policing the pledge of office is given to the Northern Ireland Assembly. The Northern Ireland Act permits the Assembly to exclude a Minister or junior Minister from office for a period of twelve months if he/she no longer enjoys the confidence of the Assembly. Such a no confidence motion can be on the grounds either that the Minister is no longer committed to non-violence and peaceful and democratic means or because of any other failure to observe the terms of office.[91] A motion of no confidence of this kind cannot be introduced without a number of formalities that are specified in the Act. Thus the motion must be introduced by the First Minister and Deputy First Minister or by the Presiding Officer. The Secretary of State may require the Presiding Officer to move such a motion. The motion must have the support of 30 MLAs and it requires cross community support.

These provisions create a kind of personal responsibility or accountability that is absent from either the Welsh or the Scottish arrangements. They are procedures designed to reassure in particular the unionist community that members of Sinn Fein, some of whom will inevitably participate in the Northern Ireland Executive for the foreseeable future, have renounced the use of violence. Their inclusion would not make sense in a Scottish or Welsh context.

Accountability—the Scottish model

The Scottish model is more recognisably similar to the Westminster model than either the Northern Irish or the Welsh models. The model is based on a distinction between the functions of the Scottish Parliament and the functions of the Scottish Executive. The First

---

[88] Northern Ireland Act, s.16.
[89] Northern Ireland Act, s.18(8).
[90] Northern Ireland Act, s.19(3)(b).
[91] Northern Ireland Act, s.30.

Minister is elected by the Parliament and his/her choice of Ministers must be approved by it. The Scottish government of the day would normally be made up members of the political party winning most seats in the Parliament. This parliamentary model is one that is based on Westminster. Scottish Ministers have similar functions in a Scottish context as Ministers of the Crown in a United Kingdom context. Their relationship to the respective Parliaments is similar. It is not surprising then, that the Scottish Executive has borrowed a number of principles from Westminster regarding the relationship between Ministers and Parliament.

Experience at Westminster has shown the need for codes of conduct for ministers in relation to their dealings with parliament, particularly in relation to the need for ministers to give as full and as truthful an account as possible. Guidance to Ministers of the Crown provides that "it is of paramount importance that Ministers give accurate and truthful information to Parliament". Inadvertent errors are to be corrected "at the earliest possible opportunity" and "ministers who knowingly mislead Parliament will be expected to offer their resignation to the Prime Minister". Ministers are also expected to be "as open as possible with Parliament" with the only ground for refusing to give information being the public interest.[92] What is or is not a matter of the public interest is defined by any relevant statute or the Government's Code of Practice on Access to Government Information.[93]

This approach has been replicated in Scotland. A Code of Conduct for Scottish Ministers was adopted in July 1999.[94] The Scottish Code, like its United Kingdom counterpart, is not a legally binding Code and there is no requirement in the Scotland Act for the adoption of such codes. Unlike the Northern Ireland Act, Ministers are not required to affirm their acceptance of the Code of Practice before taking up office. The Code does not define accountability of Ministers but it does state that "Ministers have a duty to the Parliament to account, and be held to account, for the policies, decisions and actions taken within their field of responsibility".[95] The

---

[92] *Guidance to Ministers of the Crown* can be found on the Cabinet Office web site http://www.cabinet-office.gov.uk/central/1997/mcode/p01.htm.

[93] *The Home Office Code on Access to Government Information* can be found on the Home Office web site http://www.homeoffice.gov.uk/foi/ogcode982.htm.

[94] The *Scottish Ministerial Code* can be found on the Scottish Executive web site http://www.scotland.gov.uk/library2/doc03/smic-00.htm.

[95] Para. 1.1(b).

Code recognises the "paramount importance of providing accurate and truthful information to the Parliament" and Ministers who "knowingly mislead the Parliament will be expected to offer their resignation to the First Minister".[96] Ministers should be open with the Parliament and the public and refuse to disclose information only when it is in the public interest.[97] Ministers should also require their civil servants to be as helpful as possible in giving evidence to parliamentary committees.[98]

Thus far the Scottish Code and the United Kingdom Code are in similar terms. However, the Scottish Code does introduce some purely Scottish elements reflecting the principles recommended by the CSG.[99] The first principle is power-sharing, a term more familiar in a Northern Irish context than in Scotland. In Scotland the principle of power sharing is however given a different meaning. The principle of power sharing means that the Scottish Parliament "should embody and reflect the sharing of power between the people of Scotland, the legislators and the Scottish Executive". The consequence of this principle in term of accountability is that "the Scottish Executive should be accountable to the Scottish Parliament and the Parliament and the Scottish Executive should be accountable to the people of Scotland". Accountability of the Scottish Executive to the Scottish people, arising out of the concept of power sharing, is a more nuanced approach to the concept of accountability than is familiar in traditional constitutional law terms.

The Scottish Executive has also adopted a Code of Practice on Access to Scottish Executive Information. This Code is borrowed almost directly from the equivalent United Kingdom Code but tailored to Scottish needs. Under this kilted version, Scottish Ministers may refuse to divulge information which is against the public interest. The public interest may outweigh the duty to provide information in the following areas; matters relating to defence, security and international relations; information whose disclosure would jeopardise the frankness and candour of internal discussion; communications with the royal household; matters relating to law enforcement and legal proceedings; immigration and nationality; effective management of the economy and collection of taxes or of

---

[96] Para. 1.1(c).
[97] Para. 1.1(d).
[98] Para. 1.1(e).
[99] Para. 3.1.

the public service; public appointments and honours; voluminous or vexatious requests; information which is about to be published; research data; privacy of an individual; a third party's commercially sensitive information or information given in confidence. In all these cases there is a presumption that information will be provided but that presumption may be over-ridden by the public interest.

These two Scottish Codes do not sit easily together. Principles of power sharing do not lend themselves to practices that restrict information to the people of Scotland on the grounds of a widely defined concept of public interest. Nor does the view that Ministers and civil servants may choose what to disclose sit well with principles of openness and accessibility. These matters are currently under debate in Scotland where a Scottish Freedom of Information Bill is proposed. Once it is passed the Freedom of Information Act will replace the Code of Conduct on Access to Information and will hopefully reconcile rules on access to information with the principles outlined in the Scottish Ministerial Code.

Asymmetrical or haphazard devolution?

It is difficult to escape the conclusion, in comparing the functions of the three elected bodies in the key areas of legislative powers and scrutiny of the administration, that devolution is indeed asymmetrical. Indeed there are no clear points of comparison—even the language used in the legislation is given different meanings. A reserved power in Scotland is not the same as a reserved power in Northern Ireland. There are differences in the form of devolution. On the one hand in Scotland and Northern Ireland there is legislative devolution whereas in Wales there is executive devolution. Principles of accountability differ between the institutions. Again the Welsh model is profoundly different from the other two. There are significant differences between the Northern Ireland Assembly and the Scottish Parliament in terms of personal responsibility to the underlying principles of the devolution settlement. Northern Irish Ministers must affirm their allegiance to principles underlying devolution. Procedural safeguards are more stringent in Northern Ireland in relation to human rights and equality than in Scotland or Wales. It is clear that each region has been treated on its own merits without a real regard for establishing basic ground rules. Devolution is without a logical framework and baseline.

This approach cannot truly be described as asymmetrical. An asymmetrical system is one where there is a basic pattern and where some aspects might be out of line. Devolution in the United Kingdom to date cannot be described in this way without doing an injustice to those countries where the allocation of powers to regional governments is indeed asymmetrical. Devolution in the United Kingdom is based on a number of different factors and each settlement is almost entirely different. A more logical description is haphazard devolution or at the very least the recognition that in the United Kingdom we not have not so much multi-level governance but mult-textured governance.[1]

---

[1] These ideas are taken up in Chapter 7.

Chapter 4

The Executives

Introduction

This chapter explores the structural and functional differences between the executive branch of government in Scotland, Wales and Northern Ireland. In this area there are very pointed differences between the three devolution settlements. In all three devolution settlements, the executive is drawn from the ranks of the elected representatives. After this bland statement, any similarities begin to fade. In Wales, the First Secretary and the other Secretaries chosen by him/her exercise powers delegated to them by the Assembly as a whole.[1] They are members of the committees whose structure is outlined in Chapter 2 and work with other Assembly Members in formulating and implementing policy. In Scotland and Northern Ireland powers are transferred to Ministers from Ministers of the Crown and can be conferred in subsequent legislation adopted either by Westminster or by the relevant regional parliamentary body. In Scotland, Ministers are accountable to the committees of the Parliament but they are not members of them. In Northern Ireland, statutory committees advise and assist each Minister in the formulation of policy. In each case, therefore, the relationship between the executive and the parliamentary bodies is different. In Scotland and Northern Ireland however, in law, the respective cabinets can more nearly be described as the "hub of the legislative and executive arm" than can the Welsh Assembly Cabinet.[2]

---

[1] See Chapter 3 above.
[2] I. Loveland, *Constitutional Law,* (London: Butterworths, 1996) at 335.

In Scotland and Wales, the executive branch has to command sufficient support in the parliamentary body. Difficult as this may be in a system where the scheme of proportional representation makes it virtually impossible for any one party to achieve an overall majority, the problems fade into insignificance where the executive, as is the case in Northern Ireland, is required to be inclusive of two very different community traditions and to command the support not just of a majority of members of the Assembly but to have parallel support within the parliamentary body. Furthermore, in Northern Ireland, the role of leader of the executive is shared between the First Minister and the deputy First Minister, a bicephalous arrangement that has no comparison elsewhere in the United Kingdom.

One of the major consequences of devolution has been the enormous increase in size of government in the United Kingdom in terms of individuals holding Ministerial positions. In these terms, the executive arm of government in Scotland, Wales and Northern Ireland has expanded by at least 300 per cent. Whilst some of this increase may be justified on efficiency grounds, there are clearly other reasons at play. For example, in the case of Northern Ireland there is a need to allow both community traditions to have a presence in government.

This chapter explores some of the issues surrounding the nature of cabinet government under devolution. It begins by describing the executive branches of government in Scotland, Wales and Northern Ireland. The method of selection of the executive branch in each case is determined by legislation. So too is the extent of the powers wielded by the executive. Issues of accountability and responsibility are as important to the working of devolved government as they are to the United Kingdom government. The devolution legislation does not govern the precise working relationships between executive and parliamentary bodies but provides a framework in which conventions are beginning to be established. This chapter raises the question as to how far existing constitutional conventions, in particular the key issue of collective ministerial responsibility, can be transposed to the devolved governments.[3]

---

[3] Issues relating to individual responsibility have been discussed in the previous chapter.

Scotland

In Scotland, the First Minister is nominated by the Scottish Parliament from amongst the numbers of MSPs and appointed by Her Majesty.[4] This aspect of the legislation was designed to ensure the direct accountability of the head of the executive to Parliament. The Scotland Act does not specifically state that an election must be held to choose the First Minister, it merely states that a nomination must be made. Quite obviously the First Minister must be in a position to command the support of a sufficient number of MSPs to get government business through. As is clear from the figures from the first election to the Scottish Parliament discussed in Chapter 2, no political party won an overall majority of seats. The largest party, Labour, was then faced with the choice of trying to govern with a minority government or by entering into an agreement with another party so as to secure an overall majority. Labour entered into a "Partnership for Scotland Agreement" with the Scottish Liberal Democrats. This effectively created a coalition government.[5] As part of this agreement, Donald Dewar (Labour) secured the nomination for the post of First Minister and Jim Wallace (Liberal Democrat) as deputy First Minister. During a period of illness of the First Minister the Deputy First Minister took over as head of the Scottish Executive. The constitutional position of this arrangement was disputed at the time by those who believed that a member of the Labour Party should stand in for the First Minister.

However, as other candidates came forward for the post of First Minister, elections were held. In the elections there were four candidates, each duly proposed and seconded by MSPs as required by Standing Orders. Given the number of candidates the winner had to obtain a number of votes exceeding those obtained by all the other candidates. If there had been but one candidate, he/she could have been elected by obtaining a simple majority of the votes cast. If there had been two candidates, the winning candidate would have been the one obtaining most votes. One quarter of MSPs had to vote to make the election valid. The results of the election were as follows[6]:

---

[4] Scotland Act s.45.

[5] The text of the Partnership for Scotland document can be found on http://www.scotlibdems.org.uk/docs/coalition.htm.

[6] The Presiding Officer abstained as required under Standing Orders, one MSP was absent and one Liberal Democrat abstained from voting in protest against the coalition agreement.

Denis Canavan (Independent)   3
Donald Dewar (Labour)   71
David McLetchie (Conservative)   17
Alex Salmond (SNP)   35

Donald Dewar was duly elected having received more votes than the other candidates combined. He was then able to choose his ministerial team.

There is no reference in the Scotland Act to a Scottish Cabinet as such. The Act uses the terms "Scottish Executive" and "Scottish Administration" and both these terms are wider than the traditional meaning given to the cabinet as an institution.[7] The Scottish Administration is the collective term used to cover the Scottish Executive with its supporting departmental and administrative structures. The Scottish Executive is the First Minister, Scottish Ministers appointed by the First Minister with the approval of the Parliament[8] and the Lord Advocate and Solicitor General. In addition the Act allows for the appointment of junior Scottish Ministers to assist the Scottish Ministers.[9] Junior Scottish Ministers are not part of the Scottish Executive although they are part of the Scottish Administration.

Despite the absence of the term "cabinet" in the Act, the Scottish Office press release announced Donald Dewar's nominations for those individuals he wished "to serve in the Cabinet of the Labour/Liberal Democrat Partnership Government". In effect this is a list of nominations for the posts of Scottish Ministers. The list does not, however, include the name of the Solicitor General who is, therefore, a member of the Scottish Executive, as defined in the Scotland Act, but not a member of the Cabinet.[10]

As Secretary of State for Scotland, Donald Dewar was served by a team of five ministers with responsibilities for: education; industry; agriculture, environment and fisheries; home affairs and devolution; and health and culture. The Scottish law officers, the Lord Advocate and the Solicitor General were also of ministerial rank.

---

[7] Scotland Act s.44.
[8] Scotland Act s.47.
[9] Scotland Act s.49.
[10] The roles of the Lord Advocate and the Solicitor General are discussed in Chapter 6 below.

As First Minister, Donald Dewar has a team of ten in his Scottish Cabinet. In making his nominations he created a new departmental structure with several new ministries. Cabinet Ministers have responsibility for: justice; communities (local government, housing, social inclusion); transport and environment; health and community care; rural affairs, children and education; enterprise and lifelong learning; finance. The Lord Advocate and the chief whip are also members of the cabinet. In addition to the First Minister and the ten members of the Scottish Cabinet there are ten junior Scottish Ministers each assisting in one of the ministries.

The political composition of the cabinet reflects the Labour/Liberal Democrat coalition. The Liberal Democrats secured the position of Deputy First Minister and another cabinet post (currently rural affairs). Two junior ministerial posts are reserved for the minority party.

The total ministerial team under devolution (excluding the two law officers) is therefore 18 plus the First Minister. By comparison with the size of the former Scottish Office, this is an enormous ministerial team. Of course it could be said that numbers as such tell us little about the workings of a Parliament or a government and this is to some extent true. The size of government depends on the functions that the government has to perform but it is telling that functions previously performed by a much smaller ministerial team have been taken over by a vastly expanded governmental machine.

Nineteen of the 129 MSPs are part of the executive or approximately one in seven members.[11] One of the reasons underlying the need to restrict the numbers of members of a parliamentary body from holding ministerial offices is undoubtedly one of cost but it is also one of principle. There is a need to avoid the abuse of a system of patronage. The first "modern" Prime Minister of the United Kingdom, Walpole, is generally held to be one of the first politicians to recognise the benefits of a system of patronage to a government that needed to exercise control of a parliamentary institution. Mackenzie, for example, states that Walpole used the distribution of placements, in default of a well developed party system in the early eighteenth century, to make a system of ministerial government work. He goes on to state that "the effect of his (Walpole's) system was not to corrupt the members in the sense that he was able to buy

---

[11] This is roughly the same proportion as in the Westminster Parliament.

their consciences—most of them were too rich and too independent to be so treated—but it did enable him to maintain some kind of loyalty and coherence among his supporters".[12]

In the new Scottish settlement the party system has proved insufficient to deliver support for the executive given that the largest political party does not have a majority in the chamber. The need to find places for the minority party in the coalition government as well as the need to satisfy demands from factions inside the Labour Party is at least an echo of the eighteenth century need for pragmatism displayed to such useful effect by Walpole. Donald Dewar, in deciding on his ministerial team was searching for coherence as well as loyalty. These factors, as much as the desire for good and efficient government, must have impelled him to create multiple ministries. This raises at least a question about the extent to which the parliamentary process may be subverted in the interest of a strong executive in Scotland. With so many MSPs having a personal interest in supporting the executive in addition to understandable party loyalties there is a need to be vigilant about the degree of control that is exercised by the Scottish Executive over the new Parliament. In this sense, numbers do matter. The new politics promised under devolution was supposed to herald the dawn of a more accountable form of government where the executive was to be controlled by the parliamentary institutions and not vice versa.

Before the First Minister could recommend his team to Her Majesty for appointment, they had to be approved by the Scottish Parliament.[13] No procedures exist to allow the Parliament adequate scrutiny of the ministerial team and it was inevitable that the Scottish Ministers would be approved. In the absence of adequate procedures for scrutiny, for example the holding of hearings on individual ministerial appointments in the way that the European Parliament holds hearings before Commissioners are appointed, the right of the Parliament to approve the appointment of Scottish Ministers is attenuated. In practice, as long as the First Minister can command a majority in the Scottish Parliament, the Scottish First Minister effectively has the same power to appoint his/her Scottish Cabinet as the Prime Minister has to appoint the United Kingdom Cabinet.

---

[12] K. Mackezie, *The English Parliament* (Harmondsworth: Penguin Books, 1965) at 83.
[13] Scotland Act s.47(2).

Wales

In the Welsh election, no political party won an overall majority of seats. As in Scotland, Labour was the biggest party in the National Assembly for Wales and Alun Michael opted to govern as a minority government. This was made possible by an informal agreement between Plaid Cymru and Labour to work in partnership on matters of common concern. Plaid Cymru would not automatically oppose proposals but would work constructively. This was the approach taken by the other smaller parties in Wales. The result was that Alun Michael was elected unopposed as First Secretary on May 12, 1999.

The appointment of the Welsh Cabinet follows a different procedure from that followed in Scotland. The Government of Wales Act states that the First Secretary shall appoint Assembly Secretaries and thereafter their names are to be notified to the members of the Assembly.[14] The Assembly therefore has no role in the appointment procedure. However, the First Secretary is constrained by the Government of Wales Act and the standing orders in the number of appointments that he/she can make. The Government of Wales Act specifies that standing orders can specify a maximum number of appointments to the post of Assembly Secretary. Standing Orders state that there can be no more than nine members of the Assembly Cabinet including the First Secretary.[15] One of the members of the Cabinet must have responsibility for finance and another must be the Assembly Business Manager. The First Secretary may then appoint up to six other Assembly Secretaries and must allocate to them accountability in one or more of the fields in which the Assembly has functions. Accountability is defined in the Act as meaning that the Assembly Secretary is "the member of the executive committee (now known as the Assembly Cabinet) accountable to the Assembly . . . for the exercise of the Assembly's functions in that field, except for the exercise of functions by the executive committee". The First Secretary is responsible to the Assembly for actions of the Assembly Cabinet.

---

[14] Government of Wales Act s.53.
[15] *Standing Orders for the National Assembly for Wales* were made by the Secretary of State under s.50(3) of the Government of Wales Act . They are available on the National Assembly for Wales web site at http://www.assembly.wales.gov.uk/works/standing orders/standingorders_e.htm.

Alun Michael notified the Assembly of his first Cabinet on May 12, 1999. In addition to himself, the first Welsh Cabinet was composed of eight Assembly Secretaries with accountability for: economic development; education to 16; health and social services; post 16 education and training; agriculture and the rural economy; environment (including local government and planning); finance. In addition the Business Manager or Chief Whip is also a member of the cabinet.

With the change of leadership in Wales, the new First Secretary reorganised this Cabinet structure. Rhodri Morgan retained his position as Secretary responsible for Economic Development and combined this with his role of First Secretary. He then brought in a new member of the Cabinet and split responsibilities for the environment. In addition he appointed three junior Assembly Secretaries. There is no provision in the Government of Wales Act for this category of Assembly Secretaries so these appointments have no legal status.[16]

The Assembly is required to set up subject committees that mirror the division of accountabilities of the Assembly Secretaries (except for the Business Manager and Finance Secretary).[17] Each Assembly Secretary will be a member (but cannot be the chair) of the relevant subject committee and will be required to provide the committee with information on the policies being pursued by the Assembly Cabinet in the particular field.

The overall size of the executive team in Wales is smaller than in Scotland. However the ratio of members of the Cabinet plus junior Assembly Secretaries is about one in five. Some of the same fears about the power of patronage inevitably arise in the Welsh context as arise in the Scottish. However, this issue is less pertinent in Wales where the traditional distinction between Parliament and executive does not apply. The Assembly Cabinet is very much larger than the former Welsh office team. Immediately prior to devolution, the Secretary of State for Wales led a ministerial team of two Parliamentary Under Secretaries of State. This is a quadrupling of the number of persons holding "ministerial" office.

---

[16] The Government of Wales Act specifies that the First Secretary and Assembly Secretaries are Crown servants for the purpose of the Official Secrets Act. Junior Assembly Secretaries are not provided for in the Act.

[17] Government of Wales Act s.57.

Northern Ireland

The enormously complex task of attempting to create inclusive government in Northern Ireland has led to the adoption of a system of selecting the executive which differs in very fundamental ways from that used in Scotland or Wales, or indeed from the United Kingdom. The principles underlying both the choice and the method of operation of the executive branch of government in Northern Ireland were set out in the Belfast Agreement.[18] These principles can be summarised as follows:

- allocation of ministerial portfolios must be in proportion to party strength in the Assembly

- executive authority is to be discharged on behalf of the Assembly by a First Minister and Deputy First Minister with up to ten Ministers having Departmental responsibilities

- The First Minister and Deputy First Minister must be jointly elected by the Assembly voting on a cross-party-basis, *i.e.* on the principle of parallel consent with a majority of members present and voting, including a majority of the unionist and nationalist delegations present and voting

- Ministerial posts are to be allocated to parties on the basis of the d'Hondt system by reference to the number of seats each party has in the Assembly

- All Ministers must affirm a Pledge of Office including a commitment to democratic politics and a renunciation of violence.

These principles were translated into the Northern Ireland Act which creates a bicephalous post of leader of the executive, the First Minister and Deputy First Minister.[19] These two posts are intertwined so much so that the Assembly must elect individuals to both posts at the same time. Each individual standing for one of these posts must stand jointly with the other and both must obtain the parallel consent of members of the Assembly. One cannot take up office without both having first taken the Pledge of Office and when

---

[18] *Agreement Reached in Multi-party Negotiations* Cm 4292 (1998).
[19] Northern Ireland Act s.16.

one resigns by tendering his/her resignation the other ceases to hold office but may continue to exercise his/her functions until an alternative person is elected.

This system is designed to meet the specific desire to move away from majoritarian politics in Northern Ireland and towards inclusive government based on partnership between the two competing traditions of unionism and nationalism. It is only one in a series of safeguards within the executive and results in a shared leadership role. Perhaps the surprise is that it seemed so very easy for the Assembly to elect its leadership. The Assembly met in July 1998 and elected David Trimble as First Minister (Designate) and Seamus Mallon as Deputy First Minister (Designate).

The second stage in the creation of the executive proved to be much more difficult. The multi-party Agreement had determined that the First Minister and Deputy First Minister and up to ten Ministers should discharge executive authority on behalf of the Assembly. It was for the Assembly to debate the number of Departments to which Ministers would be assigned. In February 1999 the Assembly agreed to proposals put to it by the First Minister and Deputy First Minister that there would be ten departments each headed by a Minister.[20] Standing Orders needed also to be adopted by the Secretary of State determining how the Ministers should be nominated.

However, political events overtook legal events in the following months. There appeared to be no movement on the issue of decommissioning and the bombing in Omagh indicated to many unionists that the IRA was not committed to the political process and decommissioning of terrorist weapons took centre stage. The Ulster Unionists argued that decommissioning was a prior condition to the formation of an executive and Sinn Fein retaliated that this approach was contrary to the Agreement reached on Good Friday 1998. A number of deadlines were set and missed culminating in the failure of the Assembly to nominate Ministers on the appointed day, July 15, 1999.[21]

The Assembly had been summoned to meet by the Secretary of State. However, the Ulster Unionist Party, led by the First Minister

---

[20] The restructuring of the former Northern Ireland Office into the new departmental structure was effected by the adoption of S.I. 1999 N.283 (N.I.1), Departments (Northern Ireland) Order 1999. The Order was made in February 1999 but came into effect on the day after the appointed day for devolution (December 2, 1999).

[21] Northern Ireland Assembly Official Record Thursday July 15, 1999.

(Designate), David Trimble, refused to attend the Assembly. In the absence of the Ulster Unionists, the running of the d'Hondt formula for the appointment of Ministers degenerated into a farce. What should have happened was that the nominating officer of each political party, in the order provided by standing orders, would select a ministerial office and nominate a person to hold that office. The nominee must be a person who was a member of that party and a member of the Assembly. The Presiding Officer had no choice but to follow this procedure despite the fact that, fifteen minutes before the session started, he had received a revised standing order from the Secretary of State to the effect that Ministers could only continue to hold office in the executive if the executive contained at least three unionist and three nationalist members. Of course there were no nominations from the largest political party, the Ulster Unionists. Ministers from the SDLP and Sinn Fein were duly nominated and accepted the posts offered to them. However, no executive could be formed given that there were no unionists in the putative executive.

The Deputy First Minister, Seamus Mallon, then resigned. According to the terms of the Northern Ireland Act this would also mean that the First Minister would be forced to demit office. However the Presiding Officer ruled that as the Assembly was meeting under the terms of the Northern Ireland (Elections) Act that David Trimble's position was not affected by the resignation of the Deputy First Minister. At this stage devolution to Northern Ireland appeared to have reached an impasse. The Assembly was dissolved by the Secretary of State and the process went into review. In the debate that day, David Ervine of the PUP stated that the political process in Northern Ireland was dead.

However, following Senator Mitchell's review, the political process was revived and the Assembly was summoned to meet on November 29, 1999 for the purpose of debating the resignation of the Deputy First Minister and to nominate ministers according to the d'Hondt formula.[22] A lengthy debate took place as to whether Seamus Mallon had actually resigned in July or had merely offered his resignation to the Assembly. It was clear that this debate was not an attack on the position of Mr Mallon but on Mr Trimble since the clear implication was that if Mr Mallon had indeed resigned then Mr Trimble would go down with him. Those Unionists who were opposed to accepting

---

[22] Northern Ireland Assembly Official Record Monday November 29, 1999.

the outcome of Senator Mitchell's review wanted to bring down Mr Trimble arguing that whilst Mr Mallon would get cross party support Mr Trimble would not. In the event the Assembly resolved by 71 to 28 "that this House wishes, notwithstanding his offer of resignation as Deputy First Minister, that Seamus Mallon MP hold office as Deputy First Minister (Designate)". Fifteen minutes before the commencement of the debate, the Secretary of State had amended standing orders to state that a majority of those present and voting was sufficient to allow the Assembly to resolve not to accept the offer of resignation. This was to avoid having to meet the requirement of parallel consent that would have been required in a re-election.

The Presiding Officer then ran the d'Hondt formula to nominate ministers for the Executive. That formula, which takes the number of seats gained by a political party and divides it by the number of ministerial posts held by that party plus one, gave the UUP and the SDLP three posts, and the DUP and Sinn Fein two posts. Each party had to nominate a post and a Minister in the order dictated by the formula. This means that no one particular party could necessarily gain the ministries of their choice. The results, in the order in which nominations were taken, were as follows:

Party	Ministry	Member
UUP	Enterprise, Trade and Investment	Reg Empsey
SDLP	Finance and Personnel	Mark Durkan
DUP	Regional Development	Peter Robinson
Sinn Fein	Education	Martin McGuinness
UUP	Environment	Sam Foster
SDLP	Higher and Further Education, Training and Employment	Sean Farren
DUP	Social Development	Nigel Dodds
UUP	Culture, Arts and Leisure	Michael McGimpsey
Sinn Fein	Health, Social Services and Public Safety	Bairbre deBrun
SDLP	Agriculture and Rural Development	Brid Rodgers

The Northern Ireland executive is therefore evenly balanced between unionists and nationalists. The executive is multi-party and relies on the support not of the majority of Assembly members but on cross party support. The operation of the executive is complicated by the refusal of the two DUP members to co-operate with Sinn Fein. Peter Robinson, in accepting office explained his position to the Assembly. He re-iterated his opposition to the Belfast Agreement and to the release of paramilitary prisoners but, in accepting office, he stated that he would be scrupulously fair in exercising his responsibilities. The DUP Ministers since that time have not attended cabinet meetings and have boycotted the inaugural meeting of the North South Ministerial Council.

The nature of cabinet government under devolution

Unlike the United Kingdom cabinet, described by Loveland as a "creature of convention", the executive branch of the devolved governments are very much creatures of statute.[23] More than that, they are "designer cabinets", tailored to suit very different constitutional settlements. In both Scotland and Northern Ireland there is a form of cabinet government recognisable to anyone familiar with cabinet government in the United Kingdom in that an executive is formed from out of the legislature. The executive is then accountable to the legislature for its actions. This is possible in Scotland and Northern Ireland because both legislative and executive powers have been devolved. In Wales, members of the Assembly Cabinet are accountable to the Assembly for the exercise of the Assembly's functions. In other words, Assembly Secretaries exercise powers on behalf of the Assembly. The terminology used reflects this distinction. There are ministers in Scotland and Northern Ireland and Secretaries in Wales. Assembly Secretaries have no powers attaching to their posts. Any powers exercised by the Secretaries are exercised on behalf of the Assembly.

This point is reinforced by an examination of the way in which powers have been transferred. In Scotland, functions previously exercised by Ministers of the Crown, including those previously exercised by the Secretary for State for Scotland have been transferred to the Scottish Ministers in so far as they are within devolved competence.[24] Devolved competence being broadly defined as being

---

[23] Loveland cited in note 2.
[24] Scotland Act s.53.

within those areas falling within the legislative competence of the Scottish Parliament.[25] This general transfer of ministerial functions is hedged about with exceptions for specific powers and functions detailed either in the Scotland Act itself or in subordinate legislation.[26] Nonetheless there has been a general transfer of ministerial functions from Ministers of the Crown to the Scottish Ministers. A similar general transfer of powers has been made to the Northern Irish Ministers. Ministerial functions can be conferred by an Act of the Northern Irish Assembly or by a pre-commencement legislation.[27] In the latter case, powers previously exercised by Northern Ireland's departments continue to be exercised by those departments. In relation to transferred matters, prerogative or other executive functions are to be exercised by any Northern Irish Minister or department. Contrast this approach with that taken in relation to Wales.

The powers of the Assembly are set out in Part II (sections 21–33) of the Government of Wales Act. Before these powers could be exercised a transfer of ministerial functions from Ministers of the Crown to the Welsh Assembly had to be effected. The Government of Wales Act required the Secretary of State, before the first elections, to place a draft transfer order before both Houses of Parliament making provision for the transfer of functions. The National Assembly for Wales (Transfer of Functions) Order 1999 was made in March 1999 and came into force on July 1 of that year.[28] In effect, this Order enumerates all the functions that are being transferred. Section 2 of the Order brings into force Schedule 1 which is a list of Acts of the Westminster Parliament, the earliest being the School Sites Act 1841 and the most recent the National Minimum Wage Act 1998. It also contains a list of Local and Private Acts and some

---

[25] Scotland Act s.54.
[26] Scotland Act s.56 relates to shared powers. S.57 retains the powers of Ministers of the Crown to adopt secondary legislation for the purpose of implementing and observing Community obligations despite the transfer of powers to the Scottish Ministers. Additional powers can be transferred to facilitate the devolved exercise of a devolved power. For examples of the further refinement of the general transfer S.I. 1999/1592 The Scotland Act 1998 (Concurrent Functions) Order 1999; S.I. 1999/1748 The Scotland 1998 Act (Functions Exercisable in or as regards Scotland) Order 1999; S.I. 1999/1750 The Scotland Act 1998 (Transfer of Functions to the Scottish Ministers) Order: 1999 S.I. 1999/1756 The Scotland Act 1998 (Modification of Functions) Order 1999.
[27] Northern Ireland Act s.22.
[28] S.I. 1999/672. The first general transfer order was amended by S.I. 2000/253.

Statutory Instruments. These Acts all delegate powers to Ministers of the Crown and these powers are transferred by Section 2 to the National Assembly for Wales in so far as they relate to Wales. Additional powers will be transferred to the National Assembly for Wales each time new legislation is enacted governing Welsh matters.

Certain functions are to be exercised solely by the Assembly and others by the Assembly concurrently with a Minister of the Crown. These exceptions are specified in Schedule 1. Where it is not possible to separate out the Welsh element in relation to the operation of cross border bodies functions are concurrent with the Minister although there may be transfer of some functions to the Assembly over certain English border issues. Certain functions are not to be transferred. In particular the Assembly cannot make commencement orders and the functions of the Lord Chancellor and the Attorney General are not transferred. Functions of the Comptroller and Auditor General are transferred to, or also become functions of, the Auditor General for Wales. Where a transfer is effected then all functions are transferred including those under any scheme or regulations created under the parent act. Where an enactment requires more than one Minister of the Crown to exercise a function and where the transfer order does not transfer the functions of all the Ministers then the Assembly cannot exercise the function otherwise than in accordance with the joint action requirements.

A second schedule to the Order lists functions exercisable by a Minister of the Crown. Constraints are placed on the exercise of these functions making them exercisable only either with the agreement of the Assembly or after consultation with it in so far as the functions are exercisable in relation to Wales or, where relevant, in relation to Welsh controlled waters.

This difference in approach reflects the very much more circumscribed powers of the National Assembly for Wales. The extensive enumeration of Acts, rather than a general transfer of functions, was required because in Wales executive devolution was the preferred option. In law, the powers previously exercised by ministers in the Welsh Office are being transferred to the Assembly. The Assembly then delegates these functions to Assembly Secretaries.

Collective responsibility

Given that, both structurally and functionally, the devolved cabinets are so very different, is it possible to apply the same constitutional principles to them as are applied to the United Kingdom cabinet? And can the same constitutional conventions apply to the operation of each of the devolved cabinets? In this context the most significant United Kingdom constitutional principle is the doctrine of collective ministerial responsibility. Loveland analyses the doctrine from the point of view of three important features: the confidence rule, the unanimity rule and the confidentiality rule. The government must enjoy the confidence of the legislature. This principle, according to Loveland, has recently come to mean that the government must resign on a motion of no confidence rather than the earlier version of the convention which would mean resignation of the government as a whole when defeated by a majority in the Commons. The unanimity rule requires all cabinet ministers to abide by decisions taken in cabinet and the resignation of an individual minister where he/she cannot accept the collective will of the cabinet on any particular issue. The confidentiality rule requires ministers not to disclose information about discussions and decisions taken within the cabinet setting.

The confidence rule

The confidence rule is based on assumptions of majoritarian politics. It assumes that the government of the day has an overall majority in the House of Commons and can use this majority to get its business through. Where a government loses its majority the normal course of action would be a dissolution of parliament, a new general election and a fresh government being appointed. Devolution is not based, however, on majoritarianism. Its basic premise is inclusiveness. Inclusiveness has been defined in terms of proportional representation in elections but also in terms of ownership of the institutions of government. In a proportional system of government, where a plurality of political parties compete, no one political party is likely to win an overall majority. Government then should be based on concepts of co-operation and collaboration. This approach is summed up in a speech given by Ron Davies in May 1996 where he said of the Labour Party in Wales "We will provide the leadership but we don't own the process".[29]

---

[29] Quoted in R. Davies MP, *Devolution: A Process Not An Event,* (Cardiff: Institute of Welsh Affairs, 1999).

From the results of the elections analysed in Chapter 2 it is clear that majoritarian politics are not an option under devolution. Although the systems of elections differ, the effect is the same. No single political party has a majority in any of the regional elected bodies. In Wales there is a minority administration, in Scotland a coalition and in Northern Ireland an artificially constructed cabinet in which all the political parties are represented. In Northern Ireland the use of the d'Hondt formula suppresses majoritarianism in government for the foreseeable future. Of course in Wales and Scotland there is a possibility that majoritarian politics can be revived in the future but this is unlikely given the numerical balance between constituency and regional members. A further factor militates against the domination of one particular party. This is the ever present nationalist voice. In all three regions there is a substantial minority of voters seeking independence from the United Kingdom. As long as this group remains in opposition, there is likely to be a serious contender for leadership of the devolved institutions.

All three devolution settlements provide for a fixed term of office of members of the relevant elected body. The executive therefore must gain the confidence of the elected body in whatever way it can. If it loses this confidence then it is not clear from the legislation what is to happen next. A motion of no confidence in the United Kingdom setting would normally lead to a new election. This is not possible where the elected body has a fixed electoral term. Instead a new configuration of ministers/secretaries must attempt to gain the confidence of the elected body. Thus the successful motion of no confidence against Alun Michael did not result in fresh elections but in the choice of new First Secretary and a slight reorganisation of the duties of Assembly Secretary. A vote of no confidence in the Scottish context would mean attempting to form a new coalition or for the Labour Party to attempt to govern as a minority party. In Northern Ireland, as the cabinet is chosen by all the political parties, a motion of no confidence would be unlikely to succeed. If it did, the d'Hondt formula would then come into play for the reappointment of the cabinet team.

In the context of devolution, therefore, the confidence rule plays a significantly different role than it does in the United Kingdom context. It ought to reinforce consensus politics rather than majoritarianism. Traditional British politics based on government and opposition are not appropriate in the devolved setting. Under the terms of this new political dispensation political parties must learn to co-operate as there is no real alternative.

The unanimity rule

It has been noted several times that the Scottish Executive is a coalition government composed of the political party having the largest number of seats acting together with the fourth largest party. Before the Executive could be formed these two parties had to reach political agreement on the terms for joint action. The Partnership for Scotland agreement covered the policy areas on which the two parties could agree but also laid down principles of collective responsibility. These principles included the right of each Minister to participate in decisions and to express their views frankly. Cabinet discussions were to remain private and decisions were to be binding on and supported by all Ministers, irrespective of their party allegiances. These principles were subsequently translated into a written *Guide to Collective Decision Making*.[30] In the Guide collective responsibility is defined exclusively in terms of the unanimity rule. It states that "The Scottish Executive operates on the basis of collective responsibility. This means that all decisions reached by Ministers, individually or collectively, are binding on all members of the Executive" (para. 1.2). The doctrine "bites after a decision has been reached" (para. 2.2) and "membership of the Executive requires [Ministers] to maintain a united front once decisions have been reached" (para. 2.2). The Guide goes on to spell out the implications of the doctrine in terms of confidentiality of discussions and of papers.

The approach taken in Scotland to the unanimity rule is very close to that taken at the United Kingdom level of government. It has additional force, however, in the context of the coalition. A coalition is a marriage of convenience for both parties and will only last as long as both parties can deliver the policies on which the coalition is based. In the Scottish context it is easy to give examples of where the coalition can deliver policy that is mutually desirable for both parties. Freedom of information legislation, land ownership issues and the reform of property law are areas where there is no real disagreement between the coalition partners. The weak link in the partnership agreement has been the issue of student tuition fees. Here the Labour Party is in a minority with all other parties in the Scottish Parliament being in favour of the abolition of fees. Should there be internal disagreement within the cabinet on this or on any other

---

[30] A Guide to Collective Decision Making (The Scottish Executive, August 1999).

issue, it is not clear whether the appropriate course of action would be for the resignation of the Liberal Democrat members or the resignation of the entire coalition cabinet. United Kingdom analogies are not helpful. Ministerial resignations in the past have arisen from disagreement over an aspect of policies being pursued by the Minister's own party. Such a possibility also exists in Scotland. A Labour Minister, for example, may find him/herself in opposition to a particular course of action and may wish to resign on the issues. However, where disagreement arises, in the coalition setting, out of the failure to achieve a joint approach then this challenges the coalition itself and in principle, therefore, should merit the resignation of the Executive as a whole. This means that a new Executive would then have to be approved by the Parliament.

In the present Northern Irish setting, it is extremely difficult to see how a unanimity rule could or should operate. As stated previously, the principle of cabinet government itself is not completely bedded down in Northern Ireland with two DUP members openly opposed to the whole devolution settlement. Yet these two Ministers remain within the cabinet and they are not expected to resign. However, it is worth challenging, at this point, the assumptions underlying the need for the unanimity rule. These rules have developed to mask disagreements within government and to allow the cabinet to appear united in the face of Parliament. Unanimity strengthens government against Parliament. However, in the Northern Irish context, it would be naive to pretend that the cabinet is united on policies. The Northern Irish cabinet is constructed on the basis of difference not unanimity. There is no need, at least at this stage, to mask these disagreements. Indeed, this would be quite wrong. Cross community support for the new government relies on consensus and openness. The unanimity rule is, therefore, inappropriate.

Of more significance than the unanimity rule are the undertakings given as part of the Pledge of Office that is given before a Minister can hold office in the Northern Ireland executive. He/she pledges "to participate with colleagues in the preparation of a programme for government" and to "operate within the framework of that programme when agreed within the Executive Committee and endorsed by the Assembly". It would only be where a Minister refuses to operate within the agreed policy that he/she could be expected to resign. Indeed removal of a Minister from office is possible in these circumstances "if he/she loses the confidence of the Assembly, voting

on a cross-community basis, for failing to meet his or her respon-
sibilities including . . . those set out in the Pledge of Office".[31]
Control over individual Ministers is therefore exercised by the
Assembly rather than within the cabinet setting.

The confidentiality rule

The confidentiality rule exists to reinforce the unanimity rule.
Essentially it means that Ministers, whilst remaining in cabinet, must
respect confidentiality of discussions. After resignation, of course, a
Minister is entitled to explain his or her resignation including the
nature of the disagreements that led to the resignation. The confidentiality rule has been accepted in Scotland in much the same way
as it operates in the United Kingdom government. The *Guide to
Collective Decision Making* reinforces the principle of privacy of
discussions and confidentiality of documents. The latter are not to be
made available to the public. At the time of writing there appears to
be no similar statement in relation to Wales or Northern Ireland.

However, there is an additional issue to be considered in discussing the confidentiality rule under devolution and this is the question
of how far the duty of confidentiality of decisions extends. It has
been rumoured in the press that both Labour and Liberal Democrat
members of the Scottish Executive have had discussions on the issue
of tuition fees with their United Kingdom colleagues, for example
with Gordon Brown, Tony Blair, or Paddy Ashdown. The decision
on tuition fees in Scotland is, of course, an internal one for the
Scottish Executive. It is impossible to tell whether there has been
overlap between discussions with party colleagues and discussions
within the context of the Scottish cabinet. If there is overlap then the
principle of confidentiality of discussions has obviously been
breached. It may be naïve to think that such an overlap would not
occur given that political parties are still organised on the United
Kingdom level. However collective responsibility at the devolved
level requires Ministers to give their first loyalty to their Ministerial
colleagues in the devolved executive and not to party colleagues in
other places. In addition, as will be seen in Chapter 5, policy

---

[31] *Agreement Reached in Multi-party Negotiations* Cm 4292 (1998) para. 25 and Northern
Ireland Act s.30.

decisions at the intra-governmental level may be taken in the context of the newly established Joint Ministerial Council. Confidentiality rules apply to the Joint Ministerial Council as a "cabinet of cabinets" but its very existence suggests that the confidentiality rule at the level of "local" cabinets will be breached.

The doctrine of collective ministerial responsibility as it is traditionally understood in the context of United Kingdom constitutional law is inappropriate as a principle to be applied across the board to the work of the devolved executives. In Scotland a version of the doctrine has been adopted in terms of the unanimity rule. However, the nature of coalition government means that the confidence rule is more problematic.

To adopt the doctrine in Northern Ireland is unthinkable. The measure of success of the newly established Northern Irish government will be how far it can take differences of view and forge them into a consensus. Open and accessible debate in these circumstances will assist rather hinder the workings of a multi-party cabinet. In any case, it is difficult to imagine the generation of Northern Irish politicians who are currently in power holding their tongues when policy differences arise. In these circumstances honesty, not secrecy, must be the best policy. Once policy has been adopted ministers agree to work together and that is entirely right otherwise government could not function at all, but there is no need for resignations over policy development.

The National Assembly for Wales is, of course, the executive and the doctrine just cannot apply to it. The purpose of an elected "parliamentary" body is to debate and air differences of view. The Assembly Cabinet is not a traditional style of cabinet and Secretaries are intended to work with their committees to develop policy. Again secrecy would undermine the workings of that structure and render the committees obsolete. Assembly Secretaries have accountability for the work of the National Assembly for Wales as a whole in their area of work and should be individually responsible. In the particular structure of the Assembly, doctrines based on a collective concept of responsibility are not appropriate.

Conclusions

What can be concluded from this? First it is clear that the executive branch of government under the three devolution settlements are not easily comparable. The structure and functioning of each one is unique. Thus the arrangements for the appointment of the Northern Ireland Executive result from the desire to create an inclusive executive based on party strength within the Northern Ireland Assembly. Here the key is power sharing between the two communities. This approach is not seen anywhere else in the devolution settlements. The Scottish arrangements are more familiar since they resemble in many respects the executive branch of government at the United Kingdom level. This explains why the Scottish Executive can borrow so freely from the United Kingdom government in terms of its Codes of Practice and in terms of concepts such as collective responsibility. Thus the Scottish Executive more closely resembles a United Kingdom Cabinet than it does the other devolved executives. The Welsh Cabinet is not a cabinet in any sense in which that word has been used in United Kingdom constitutional law. The First Secretary and his/her Assembly Secretaries exercise powers delegated to them from the National Assembly for Wales. Again this approach is unique.

In these circumstances, it is unwise to attempt to transfer over principles of constitutional law from the United Kingdom system. In particular, principles of collective responsibility are less germane than the principles of accountability discussed in the previous chapter. Individual ministerial responsibility, or even principles of personal responsibility, assume therefore far greater importance under devolution.

Chapter 5

Policy formulation

One of the effects of devolution has been to turn policy-making systems within the United Kingdom, quite literally, inside out. Decisions previously taken internally within cabinet or cabinet committees or government departments are now to be taken either within the context of separate devolved administrations or in the context of intra-governmental relations. The term "intra-governmental relations" in this sense is used to denote the links between the regional governments and the United Kingdom government and the links between the devolved governments themselves. In addition, the settlement in Northern Ireland brings into play an international dimension requiring a mechanism to co-ordinate inter-governmental relations between the United Kingdom and the Republic of Ireland and between the devolved governments and the government of the Republic of Ireland. Supporting this complex network is an equally complex web of relations between government departments operating either wholly internally to the United Kingdom or externally between United Kingdom or regional government departments and departments of the Republic of Ireland. All this is in addition to the already complex inter-governmental relations of which both the United Kingdom and the Republic of Ireland are part as members of the European Union.

There is no clear constitutional model that could be borrowed to facilitate these links. Devolution creates neither a federal nor a confederal state. Each devolution settlement differs from the next in some fundamental ways. Powers devolved to Northern Ireland are not the same as those devolved to Scotland. Wales lacks an independent legislature. Devolution is asymmetrical at best or haphazard at worst. Westminster and Whitehall have a greater or lesser part to play in some aspects of the work of the regional governments. Devolution has therefore created a multi-layered and multi-textured system of government within the United Kingdom and one which requires new institutions and frameworks in which to operate.

Lessons can without doubt be drawn from the study of the constitutional arrangements of federal states. In his study, Cornes suggests that an understanding of the theory and practice of concurrent and co-ordinate federalism would assist in understanding both the nature of the problems that might arise under devolution and could provide some solutions to them.[1] In the pure theory of co-ordinate federalism there is a clear division of responsibilities between levels of government, each level operating in its own defined sphere. More realistic in most cases is the theory of concurrent federalism where there is significant overlap between the levels of government with the consequent need for policy co-ordination.

The approach in the devolution legislation has been to transfer certain powers to the Scottish Parliament and the Northern Ireland Assembly. However, in many areas the boundary between the powers of the devolved institutions and the United Kingdom institutions is not clear. In these circumstances, it will be important to develop constitutional conventions to resist "competence creep" where competencies "accrue to central government" despite constitutional provisions that enumerate the functions of various levels of government.[2] In a United Kingdom context, where devolution is untried and untested, and where there has been increasing centralisation over the past two decades, there will be a need to resist such competence creep from the outset.

This chapter argues that to secure the devolution settlement two issues need to be confronted. The first is that the United Kingdom government must respect the devolution settlement and resist the temptation to use any of its powers legal, political or financial to encroach on the powers of the devolved institutions. However, there is a need to co-ordinate policy. This need arises because the delimitation of powers between the levels of government under the devolution settlement is not precise. In the United Kingdom devolution "is not a one-size-fits-all-solution".[3]

---

[1] R. Cornes, "Intergovernmental Relations in a Devolved United Kingdom: Making Devolution Work" in R. Hazell (ed.) *Constitutional Futures: a history of the next ten years* (Oxford: OUP 1999).

[2] D. Chalmers, *European Union Law Vol. I* (Aldershot: Dartmouth, 1998) at 232.

[3] HC Deb vol 336 col 671 October 21, 1999.

The devolution settlement has brought about a multi-layered government in the sense of creating different tiers or levels of government but it has also created a multi-textured democracy in which power is located in several levels of government at the same time. There is the possibility throughout the devolution settlement that legal competence to act might simultaneously reside in one site of power or in multiple sites. All of this is made more complex by the fact that in most of the areas where power has been devolved to the regional tier of government the central government also retains an interest since these are areas governed by international or European law, both matters reserved by the United Kingdom.

There clearly needs to be co-ordination in this structure but co-ordination of policy should not become an excuse or a mechanism for re-centralisation. In particular, principles need to be articulated to require central government to allow devolution to work.

The second issue is that the devolved institutions must operate within the context of a union state. They must not, therefore, in exercising their own devolved powers jeopardise the existence of the United Kingdom (or the Republic of Ireland as the case may be). All parties within the devolution settlement must act with restraint and with the objective of providing better government for these islands as a whole.

The context in which intra-governmental relations are to be developed is all important. In the second half of the twentieth century inter-governmental relations typically developed in the context of institutions. The creation of institutions as part of the treaty framework establishing the European Community, for example, was seen as important in that institutions could facilitate the implementation of policy and could provide a framework in which the Member States could co-operate. Institutions would have a life of their own, existing side by side but independent of the Member States. Intra-governmental relations equally require a framework. There must be a context in which policy preferences can be articulated and compromises reached. Without a level of political co-operation devolution cannot function effectively. Institutional structures of co-operation are therefore essential.

This chapter examines these issues by first examining the principles that govern intra-governmental relations within the United Kingdom. It then examines the institutional framework that has been established for the co-ordination of policy at the ministerial and the departmental level. In order to examine how these mechanisms will function, the chapter then examines how European policy is now to be co-ordinated as an example of how the scheme is intended to work.

Principles governing intra-governmental relations

The principles underlying the relationships between the United Kingdom government and the devolved administrations have been set out in a formal Memorandum of Understanding.[4] This Memorandum is agreed by all parties to be a "statement of political intent". It is said to be binding in honour alone and is not intended to create legal obligations between the parties. It is an agreement between governments and was negotiated entirely at the intra-governmental level without input from either the United Kingdom Parliament or any of the regional parliamentary bodies. It is thus an agreement between the United Kingdom government, the Scottish Ministers, the Northern Ireland Executive and the Cabinet of the National Assembly for Wales. Members of the Northern Ireland Executive as such did not, of course, take part in the negotiations, due to the delay in establishing an executive in Northern Ireland. A further point to note is that the Memorandum of Understanding binds only the Cabinet of the National Assembly for Wales despite the fact that it is the Assembly that is the executive and members of the Cabinet merely exercise delegated powers. Assembly Secretaries are not, therefore, ministers in the same way as ministers in Northern Ireland and Scotland. This is perhaps the first sign that the form of devolution in Wales is incompatible with other forms of devolution in the United Kingdom and that the modified form of cabinet government will need to move more closely to the model of legislature/cabinet that is used elsewhere.

The Memorandum of Understanding sets out five principles governing intra-governmental relations post devolution. These are:

- the principle of good communication
- the principle of co-operation
- the principle of exchange of scientific, technical and policy information

---

[4] *Memorandum of Understanding and supplementary agreements* SE/99/36 laid before the Scottish Parliament by the Scottish Ministers October 1999.

- the principle of confidentiality
- the principle of accountability.

These principles are designed to ensure that devolution does not bring with it internal political disputes by allowing for co-ordination of policy by way of information exchange, communication and consultation. The lines of government are to remain open even after devolution. It is stated that a single policy or single approach to policy will not be imposed and that each administration will have the opportunity to participate in policy formulation by allowing each administration the opportunity to make representations especially where one administrations's work may have some bearing on the work of the others.[5]

This exchange of information and consultation is set against the political agreement to co-operate "on matters of mutual interest".[6] It is difficult to imagine any policy areas where there are not matters of mutual interest particularly in social and economic matters. It may thus be the case that, post devolution, there will be separate but parallel policies pursued throughout the United Kingdom with only differences in emphasis. It would not, for example, make sense for a regional government to spend heavily on health policies at the expense of other social policies since the effect might be to create medical tourism from a region whose administration did not rate health as such a high priority. Factors militating towards similarity of policy making are enhanced where administrations are of similar political complexion.

It is perhaps implicit within the agreement to co-operate on matters of mutual interest that all administrations will work towards the success of the devolution settlement itself but this is not explicitly stated. Yet it is perhaps here more than anywhere else that there is a need to recognise an obligation of co-operation. The need for such a legally binding obligation has been recognised, albeit in a rather weak formulation, at the level of the European Union. The duty of sincere co-operation has been developed by the European Court of Justice to enforce the obligations imposed by Article 10 of the Treaty. These are obligations to "ensure fulfilment of the obligations arising out of this Treaty or resulting from action taken by the institutions".

---

[5] *Memorandum of Understanding* para. 4.
[6] *Memorandum of Understanding* para. 7.

Member States must facilitate the achievement of the Community's task and abstain from taking action that would jeopardise the attainment of the objectives of the Treaty.

There are several instances where the devolved institutions will be required to co-operate with United Kingdom institutions. For example, in negotiating a United Kingdom position in relation to European matters there will be a need to reach a common position which then becomes the agreed line.[7] Implicit in this approach is a recognition that in seeking consensus all parties will need to accept that the position reached may not always reflect the particular concerns of one region over those of another. But the corollary must be that, at the same time, no single region should seek to dominate the others, otherwise the principles underlying devolution would be negated. A duty of sincere co-operation ideally requires all parties to work together for the common good.

In the European context the duty of sincere co-operation is seen as part of the commitment of the Union and the Member States to the rule of law where the objectives of the Union are clearly expressed in the text of the treaties. There is no comparable text for the United Kingdom as a whole and there is not a complete acceptance that the maintenance of the United Kingdom as a constitutional order is or should be an objective of our constitutional law. The duty of sincere co-operation can only apply where all the parties accept the same objectives and share core values. The devolution settlement must therefore be accepted as the constitutional settlement for the United Kingdom as a whole, at least for the foreseeable future. Otherwise it cannot provide a settlement based on the acceptance of the rule of law. Where political parties seek to disrupt the devolution settlement by seeking to break away from it by way of independence, the duty of sincere co-operation is unlikely to provide a sufficiently strong counter force.

The Memorandum of Understanding is an agreement between governments. It does not and cannot dictate the way in which the

---

[7] This was the approach taken in *Scotland's Parliament* Cm 3658 (1997) 16 which states "Scottish Executive Ministers and officials should be fully involved in discussions within the U.K. government about the formulation of the U.K.'s policy position on all issues which touch on devolved matters. This will require, of course, mutual respect for the confidentiality of those discussions and adherence to the resultant U.K. line . . ." This approach is reflected in the *Concordat on Co-ordination of European Policy Issues* which is one of the supplementary agreements attached to the Memorandum of Understanding.

parliaments and assemblies will operate in the context of devolution. However, parliamentary business is of course dictated by the needs of government and one of the needs of at least the current government is that devolution should work. Thus, although both the Scotland Act and the Northern Ireland Act provide for a transfer of legislative power, this is stated to be without prejudice to the power of the United Kingdom Parliament to legislate on any matter. Should the United Kingdom Parliament choose to use its powers in this way, the devolution settlement would be dead in the water. The United Kingdom government therefore has accepted the need for it to proceed "in accordance with the Convention that the United Kingdom Parliament would not normally legislate with regard to devolved matters except with the agreement of the devolved legislature".[8] In practice the United Kingdom Parliament will not be given the opportunity to exercise its theoretical right to legislate in devolved matters. On this matter the Memorandum of Understanding reflects the guiding principle accepted by the House of Commons, in taking note of the Fourth Report on the Procedural Consequences of Devolution and the First Special Report from the Committee, that "Parliament has agreed that certain powers and responsibilities should pass from it to the devolved legislatures and parliamentary procedures and customs should not be called in aid to undermine that decision".[9]

The devolution settlement is therefore secured by convention and political agreement rather than by legally binding and justiciable constitutional norms. What is missing is a constitutional principle to bind the devolution settlement together and to provide a legal guarantee of devolved autonomy. Similar problems have arisen within the European Union where the principle of subsidiarity has been developed to protect and police the boundary between European and Member State competencies.

---

[8] Memorandum of Understanding para. 13.

[9] HC 185 (1999) *Procedure Committee's Fourth Report on the Procedural Consequences of Devolution* and HC 148 and 376 (1999) the Committee's first and second special reports. Four principles are outlined in the Report. They were summarised by Margaret Beckett in the debate on the procedural consequences of devolution HL Dec vol 336 col 606 October 21, 1999. She stated "They are, in short, that parliamentary procedures should not be called in aid to undermine the devolution settlement agreed by Parliament; that there should be minimal procedural barriers to close co-operation between MPs and Members of the devolved legislatures; that all MPs have an interest in matters that remain the responsibility of the United Kingdom Parliament and that there should be consistency in the way that the House deals with devolved legislatures. See the discussion of these issues in Chapter 3 above.

Two of the objectives of the modernisation project undertaken by New Labour are to move the process of decision making closer to the citizen and to complete the chain of democratic accountability.[10] Decentralisation of decision making is seen as an element in improving democracy and strengthening the position of the citizen.[11] Citizens will feel less remote from government and will be better able to participate in decisions affecting their lives.[12] Decentralisation as a good in itself is one aspect of the concept of subsidiarity. A former Advocate General of the European Court of Justice explains that subsidiarity is not only a "preference for the exercise of powers by the lower level of authority. It must be seen as a guideline for constitutional and ordinary legislators to *allocate* (emphasis in text) to a lower level of authority, and even as an incentive to restrict public authority as a whole".[13] In this view, decentralisation is a moral imperative on legislators to allocate decision making to the level nearest the citizen. It is clear that New Labour does not accept this version of the concept of subsidiarity in its totality. Otherwise devolution would be more widespread and certainly there would be a strong case for the devolution of legislative powers to Wales. Furthermore, the legislator would be required to state explicitly the imperatives that underlie the reservation of general or specific powers to Westminster. Subsidiarity would provide a test therefore against which to measure the reserved powers. National security, the protection of human rights, public policy, the need to uphold the rule of law or economic stability might be sufficient justification for the retention of powers to Westminster.

Subsidiarity is not, however, only a moral obligation. It has a legal content. Within the European Union subsidiarity operates as an

---

[10] See, for example, the statement in CM 3718 (1997) *A National Assembly for Wales* "By establishing the Assembly, the Government is moving the process of decision-making closer to the citizen: many more decisions about Wales will be made in Wales . . . The Welsh Assembly will complete the chain of democratic accountability running all the way from the community council through unitary local authorities and Westminster on to the European Union".

[11] See, for example, the statement by John Reid. "Devolution is about modernising the way in which we govern ourselves in this United Kingdom, decentralising power and empowering institutions". HC Deb vol 336 col 670 October 21, 1999.

[12] See, for example, Donald Dewar's preface to CM 3658 (1997) *Scotland's Parliament* "This reform . . . can . . . connect and involve people with the decisions that matter to them. It can bring a sense of ownership to political debate and a new confidence to our affairs".

[13] W. van Gerven, "Towards a Coherent Constitutional System within the European Union" (1996) 2 *European Public Law* at 91.

organising principle where the European Union and the Member States share competencies. There are certain areas of Community law where the Member States are debarred from taking unilateral action. The setting of the Common External Tariff is one such area. However, in many other areas the Member States share with the Community the power to take appropriate action, including the power to legislate. It is here that the principle of subsidiarity operates.

The most recent statement on the principle of subsidiarity in European law is found in the *Protocol on the application of the principles of subsidiarity and proportionality* annexed to the Treaty of Amsterdam. The Protocol states that the principle of subsidiarity is a guide as to how shared powers are to be exercised at Community level. Subsidiarity is said to be a dynamic concept to be applied in the light of the objectives of the Community. Because it is dynamic, subsidiarity allows for an expansion or reduction in the powers exercised at Community level at any given time. When the Community proposes to legislate, a justification must be given outlining the reason for the proposed action. This justification must be substantiated by reference to qualitative or quantitative indicators. To meet the subsidiarity principle that justification must show that the objective of the proposed measure cannot be met by the Member States and that the objectives can be better met by action taken at the European level. The Protocol gives guidelines to assist in making the decision as to whether Community level action is necessary:

- where the issue has transnational aspects that are not susceptible to national regulation,
- where the Treaty requires action to be taken at Community level or Member States interests would be damaged without Community level action
- where Community level action would produce benefits of scale or effect then the Community may assume the power to take action.
- otherwise, the power is to be exercised by the Member States.

Where action is taken at Community level such action is to be as simple as possible leaving the maximum scope for national decision. Community action should respect national arrangements and the legal orders of the Member States. Where the Commission proposes action it should consult widely, justify its proposal and take into account any burdens which it will impose. All the European institutions must take into consideration the principle of subsidiarity particularly in their role as legislators.

Commenting on this aspect of the principle of subsidiarity, Van Gerven states that this "means that all Community institutions are required to let powers which they share with national authorities *remain unused* (emphasis added) if the proposed action can be sufficiently achieved by the member States".

The principle of subsidiarity, as it has been developed at the European Union level, could provide the basis of a constitutional norm in the United Kingdom. The principle of subsidiarity would act as a self-denying ordinance on Westminster to let powers "remain unused" except in limited circumstances. Westminster or Whitehall should never act where a power has been devolved and should only act where competencies are shared or concurrent where the objective of a proposed action cannot be met by the devolved institutions and where action at the United Kingdom level is demonstrably more effective than action at the local level. The Amsterdam Protocol guidelines, with suitable amendments, are unusually apposite to such a determination. United Kingdom level institutions should only act:

- where the issue has a United Kingdom wide dimension (or possibly an international obligation requiring action at the level of central government)

- where the legislation specifically reserves a matter to the United Kingdom authorities or where one part of the United Kingdom would be adversely affected by a proposed course of action by one of the devolved administrations and

- where United Kingdom level action would produce benefits of scale or effect for all parts of the United Kingdom.

Without some form of constitutional guarantee of this kind, the underlying objective of bringing decision making closer to the citizen will be lost.

A further lesson may also be drawn from an examination of the principle of subsidiarity. This relates to the content and scope of any proposed action taken at the United Kingdom level. Subsidiarity is closely allied at the European level with the principle of proportionality. Proportionality refers not to the division of powers between levels of government but to the content of any proposed legislation or action. Article 5 of the Treaty requires that, where Community level action is taken, the action "shall not go beyond what is necessary to achieve the objectives of this Treaty". Two further restrictions in the content of Community action are found in the

Amsterdam Protocol: action taken at the Community level should respect national legal arrangements and traditions and it should provide maximum scope for action to be taken by the member states. Translating these principles into the United Kingdom context would lead to restraint on the part of the United Kingdom authorities in the content of proposed United Kingdom legislation. Framework legislation leaving choices to the devolved institutions as to how to implement the principles might be more appropriate than heavily prescriptive legislation. This approach, in particular, should be taken where primary legislation is adopted at Westminster for Wales so as to give maximum freedom for the National Assembly for Wales to decide on specifically Welsh solutions.

The Memorandum of Understanding falls short of these European principles. It is a pragmatic document promising co-operation and requiring confidentiality in return. It is far from being a sufficiently principled basis for the operation of intra-governmental relations in the devolved setting.

Institutional structures

The devolution settlements provide for the creation of a number of different structures or institutions for the co-ordination of policy. These structures are outlined briefly below. Some of them arise from the implementation of the Belfast Agreement and are part of the process of involving all levels of government within the United Kingdom in the peace process. Others involve the government of the Republic of Ireland in recognition of the need to deepen relations between both parts of Ireland and between Ireland and the United Kingdom. In addition, the Memorandum of Understanding created a Joint Ministerial Committee to meet in various formats. Co-ordination of policy is required at several levels—at ministerial level, at agency level and at departmental level.

Ministerial level institutions

JOINT MINISTERIAL COMMITTEE

The Joint Ministerial Committee was created as part of the Memorandum of Understanding discussed above. It is effectively a cabinet of cabinets. Its function is to provide "central co-ordination of the overall relationship" between the United Kingdom government and the devolved institutions.[14] The Joint Ministerial Committee is to meet in plenary session once per year.[15] This is effectively a summit level meeting bringing together, under the convenership of the Prime Minister, his/her deputy, the Scottish and Northern Irish First Ministers and Deputy First Ministers, the Welsh First Secretary and one other Assembly Secretary and the Secretaries of State for Scotland, Wales and Northern Ireland. The Joint Ministerial Committee may also meet in functional format bringing together the relevant Ministers and Secretaries, *e.g.* for environment. For these purposes the Joint Ministerial Committee is convened by the responsible United Kingdom Minister.[16]

One particularly important format for the Joint Ministerial Committee is where it meets under the convenership of the Foreign Secretary to consult on European Union matters. It is envisaged that the bulk of the work of the Joint Ministerial Committee in this format will be conducted by correspondence given the frequently short response time for European Union matters.[17]

The terms of reference of the Joint Ministerial Committee are set out in the Memorandum of Understanding.[18] It will:

- consider non-devolved matters which impinge on devolved responsibilities, and devolved matters which impinge on non-devolved responsibilities;

- with agreement between all the parties, consider devolved matters if it is beneficial to discuss their respective treatment in different parts of the United Kingdom;

- keep liaison arrangements under review

- consider disputes between the administrations.

The internal language of politics has been replaced by the language of diplomacy and negotiation. In essence the function of the Joint Ministerial Committee is to avoid having differences in approach

---

[14] *Memorandum of Understanding* para. 22.
[15] *Memorandum of Understanding, Part II Supplementary Agreements. Para. A1.3.*
[16] *Memorandum of Understanding, Part II Supplementary Agreements. Para. A1.4.*
[17] *Memorandum of Understanding, Part II Supplementary Agreements. Para. A1.9.*
[18] *Memorandum of Understanding, Part II Supplementary Agreements. Para. A1.2.*

turn into political, and therefore external, disputes. However where an issue does turn into a dispute, the Joint Ministerial Committee is also the mechanism of dispute resolution.[19] Where the dispute is a bilateral one between the United Kingdom government and a devolved administration, the Joint Ministerial Committee may meet in a bilateral format to resolve the difference under the chair of the responsible United Kingdom Minister. The relevant territorial Secretary of State may also use his/her good offices to assist in the resolution of disputes but, where these mechanisms fail, disputes are to be referred to the Joint Ministerial Committee Secretariat.[20] The Joint Ministerial Committee Secretariat is composed of officials from the United Kingdom Cabinet Office and the devolved administrations. The lead role is taken by Cabinet Office officials with responsibility to the Prime Minister but the Secretariat is required to provide impartial advice to all members of the Joint Ministerial Committee.[21]

The Joint Ministerial Committee cannot take binding decisions.[22] It is an advisory body in which frank discussion is encouraged. Confidentiality of discussions is to be observed by all participants. However, once agreement has been reached on an issue, "the expectation is that participating administrations will support" the agreed line.

The Joint Ministerial Committee shares several features with the Council of Ministers of the European Union, However, in the Council of Ministers where all ministers are treated equally, the chair rotates amongst the members. In the Joint Ministerial Committee the chair is always taken by a United Kingdom Minister, who incidentally represents English interests as well as United Kingdom interests, thus creating at least an impression, even if this is not in fact not intended to be the case, that United Kingdom Ministers control the process. It also creates the impression that the devolved administrations are intended to be subordinate rather than partners within the Joint Ministerial Committee.

The Joint Ministerial Committee structure has now been extended to set up three standing committees on child poverty, pensioner poverty and the digital revolution. In the view of the Scottish

---

[19] *Memorandum of Understanding, Part II Supplementary Agreements. Para. A1.5.*
[20] *Memorandum of Understanding, Part II Supplementary Agreements. Para. A1.7.*
[21] *Memorandum of Understanding, Part II Supplementary Agreements. Para. A2.1.*
[22] *Memorandum of Understanding, Part II Supplementary Agreements. Para. A 1.10.*

Executive these three areas are ones where it is necessary to work together "within the United Kingdom economic, fiscal and social framework" and "this means positive dialogue on policy co-ordination".[23]

The Belfast Agreement

Strands two and three of the Belfast Agreement commit the participants to creating institutions on an all Ireland basis and on a United Kingdom and Irish basis to co-ordinate policy in a number of areas. These institutions are essential parts of the overall peace agreement and are stated to be "interlocking and interdependent on one another and on the Assembly". In particular the functions of the Assembly and, the North/South Ministerial Council were said to be "so closely inter-related that the success of each depends on that of the other".[24]

North/South Ministerial Council

In its structure the North/South Ministerial Council shares many features with the Joint Ministerial Committee discussed above. Its function is to bring together Ministers from the governments of Northern Ireland and the Republic of Ireland "to develop consultation, co-operation and action within the island of Ireland".[25] The North/South Ministerial Council is to meet in plenary format twice a year. In effect these are high level bi-lateral summits led by the Taoiseach in the case of the Irish government and the First Minister and Deputy First Minister in the case of the Northern Ireland executive. Participation is the North/South Ministerial Council is one of the essential responsibilities attaching to these posts.[26] The North/South Ministerial Council will also meet in a variety of functional formats on a regular and frequent basis and in an appropriate format to discuss E.U. policy and to resolve disagreement. In discussing E.U. matters, the North/South Ministerial

---

[23] SE 1502/1999 November 29, 1999.
[24] *Agreement between the Government of the United Kingdom and the Government of Ireland establishing a North/South Ministerial Council* Cm 4294 (1999).
[25] *The Agreement reached in multi-party negotiations* Cm 4292 (1998).
[26] *The Agreement reached in multi-party negotiations* Cm 4292 (1998) Strand Two para. 2.

Council is to discuss implementation of E.U. law and policy as well as proposals under consideration within the E.U. framework. Measures will be taken (as yet unspecified) to ensure that the views of the Council are taken into account and represented appropriately at relevant E.U. meetings.

The terms of reference of the North/South Ministerial Council are set out in the Belfast Agreement. It operates in areas of mutual interest and where matters fall within the competence of both administrations. It will:

- exchange information, discuss and consult
- use best endeavours to reach agreement on the adoption of common policies, making determined efforts to overcome disagreements
- take decisions on policies for implementation separately in each jurisdiction
- take decisions on policies and actions for cross-border bodies.

The North/South Ministerial Council could not come into being until power had been devolved to Northern Ireland in December 1999. It met in transitional form on the first of December 1999 as required by the Belfast Agreement and agreed six matters for co-operation through existing bodies in each separate jurisdiction; transport, agriculture, education, health, environment and tourism. In these areas policy will require to be co-ordinated and decisions taken within the North/South Ministerial Council will need to be implemented separately but in parallel within the two jurisdictions. Six matters are to be subject to co-operation through joint cross-border bodies; inland waterways, food safety, trade and business development, special E.U. programmes, language, aquaculture and marine matters. Any changes to these arrangements need to be agreed by the North/South Ministerial Council itself, the Northern Ireland Assembly and the Oireachtas.

The first plenary session of the North/South Ministerial Council was subsequently held in Armagh on the thirteenth of December 1999. It was agreed that priority be given to meetings of the North/South Ministerial Council in sectoral format to consider issues relating to the twelve subject matters outlined above. Plenary sessions are to take place at six monthly intervals, the second being scheduled in Dublin in June 2000.

The significance of this Council can be gauged by the fact that the two DUP Ministers in the Northern Ireland Executive refused to attend the plenary and will presumably boycott any sectoral meetings of the Council. These Ministers hold portfolios on regional and social development and their lack of co-operation will jeopardise to some extent the work of the North/South Ministerial Council in these particular areas. However, this may only be a short-term problem. In the longer term, the North/South Ministerial Council provides the opportunity for allowing for policy co-ordination on an all-island basis in areas where such co-operation makes common sense. It does so whilst respecting the sovereignty of both parties. It has the further advantage of providing a framework in which confidence can be established in a non-threatening environment of mutual trust. It can be seen as a precursor to a unified governmental structure for the island of Ireland if not, as nationalists would prefer, a united Ireland itself.

British-Irish Council

The British-Irish Council had its inaugural summit on December 17, 1999. Its function, according to the Belfast Agreement, is "to provide harmonious and mutually beneficial development of the totality of relationships among the people of these islands". It will meet at summit level twice per year with representation from the British and Irish governments, from the devolved administrations and representatives of the Isle of Man and the Channel Islands. It can meet in functional format at any other time. The key to the British-Irish Council is flexibility since in addition to providing a forum for multilateral exchanges, it can also meet in bilateral format as required. Thus two or more of the members of the British-Irish Council may opt to meet together and to come to common policies and agree methods of implementing them.

The terms of reference of the British-Irish Council are as flexible as its structure. On matters of mutual interest within the competence of the relevant administrations it may:

- exchange information, discuss, consult and use best endeavours to reach agreement
- agree common policies or common actions involving all or some members

Decisions are normally to be taken by consensus but where common policies or actions are taken, then all the participating administrations must agree. The language of common policies and actions and the adoption of a principle of flexibility are reminiscent of the approach taken in the Maastricht but more specifically the Amsterdam Treaty. No definition is given of common action but it may include a mechanism for harmonising laws or administrative practices as well as taking forward policy and funding initiatives.

At the inaugural meeting, five topics were chosen as matters for early discussion, drugs, social inclusion, environment, transport and the knowledge economy. Each topic was assigned to a lead administration to take matters forward. For example, social inclusion policies were to be headed by the Scottish Executive and the Cabinet of the National Assembly for Wales. In addition, a list of 12 further topics was agreed in an indicative list of issues suitable for the work of the British-Irish Council. These include several areas that overlap with the work of the North/South Ministerial Council such as health issues, agriculture, culture and tourism and approaches to E.U. issues. In addition to these areas, there are several areas unique to the British-Irish Council such as approaches to prison and probation policies and sporting activities.

British-Irish Intergovernmental Conference

The British-Irish Intergovernmental Conference was the third inter-governmental structure agreed under the terms of Strand Three of the Belfast Agreement. It is a standing Conference of the British and Irish governments and replaces the Anglo-Irish Intergovernmental Council and Conference that had been created under the now defunct Anglo-Irish Agreement of 1985. The Conference brings together Ministers at summit level or in functional format to promote bilateral co-operation on matters of mutual interest. When non-devolved matters are to be the subject of debate within the Conference, it is co-chaired by the Irish Minister for Foreign Affairs and the British Secretary of State for Northern Ireland. The Irish government has the right to put forward views and proposals on any matter affecting Ireland. Decisions are taken by agreement with both parties making determined efforts to reach agreement.

The main area of interest of the British-Irish Council is co-operation in security matters. It has particular responsibilities in relation to rights, justice, prisons and policing. It is also to review the operation of the British-Irish Agreement and is due to report on the entirety of the agreement at the end of 2002.

Departmental level co-ordination

Writing in 1999, Pyper suggested that issues surrounding the organisation of the civil service had been "the neglected dimension of devolution".[27] He also suggests that there was concern within the civil service that the unity of the home civil service would be threatened by devolution. Indeed the logic of devolution would seem to require that separate governments should be served by separate administrations. Yet this approach has been rejected in the devolution settlements. Hazell suggests that in the long term this may be untenable with demands coming from the "Scottish and Welsh Executive to have their own civil service, like the Northern Ireland Civil Service".[28] In his research, Osmond reaches similar conclusions. He states that "the emergence of a much more distinctive Welsh machinery of government, combined with a parallel distancing of previously more intimate connections with Whitehall will further emphasise the distinctiveness of the civil service in Wales".[29] Yet both the Scotland Act and the Government of Wales Act specifically state that employment in the Scottish Administration or as a member of the Assembly staff is "service in the Home Civil Service".

Prior to devolution, Whitehall departments and the Scottish and Welsh Offices operated so as to exchange information to assist one single set of Ministers of the Crown in the formulation and implementation of policy. Post devolution, these internal mechanisms have been, to some extent, externalised, and the need for co-ordination has arisen "to take account of the interaction of devolved and reserved matters and shared interests in matters such as E.U. business".[30] The method chosen to explicate these newly externalised relationships has been the adoption of concordats.

According to Ron Davies, concordats are "not part of a carefully thought out scheme of devolution".[31] The idea behind them emerged

---

[27] R. Pyper, "The Civil Service: A Neglected Dimension of Devolution" (1999) *Public Money & Management* at 45.

[28] R. Hazell in note 1.

[29] J. Osmond, *Adrift but not afloat: the civil service and the National Assembly* (Cardiff: Institute for Welsh Affairs, 1990) at 26.

[30] B. Winetrobe, *Guidance on concordats between the Scottish Executive and UK government departments contained in Concordats*, SPICE Research Paper 99/12. This excellent research paper sets out all the major issues relating to concordats. See also O. Gay, *Devolution and Concordats*, Research Paper 99/84 House of Commons Library.

[31] National Assembly for Wales Official Record December 7, 1999 at 48.

during the process of writing the white paper and the legislation when it became clear that there was a need to "ensure that the process of government . . . at an official level, as well as on a political level, could proceed unhampered by the constitutional changes we were making". This sounds very much like an argument that devolution was not intended to disrupt the normal channels of government in the United Kingdom.

Concordats

Concordats are non-legally binding agreements setting out key aspects of the working relationships between the devolved administrations and Whitehall departments. They set the ground rules for administrative co-operation and exchange of information Concordats are defined as being "overarching" where they contain general principles governing the relationships between government departments. Overarching concordats on co-ordination of European Union policy issues, on financial assistance to industry, on international relations and on statistics were published at the same time as the Memorandum of Understanding. Subsequently bilateral concordats have been published between Whitehall departments and the devolved administrations detailing the exact responsibilities and the precise working relationships between departments. Some twenty of these bilateral concordats had been published between Whitehall and the devolved administrations with more promised to follow. It would be impossible to attempt to analyse these in any depth in this book. The approach that is taken is to attempt to see how they would influence and indeed determine the way European Union policy is formulated in the United Kingdom post devolution. This serves as an example to demonstrate how the concordats and the intra-governmental arrangements outlined above are intended to work.

European Policy Co-ordination

One way of attempting to assess how the intra-governmental mechanisms outlined above may operate in practice is to try to map out how a particular policy area might be dealt with. Relations with the European Union provide an interesting case-study given the complicated structure of the legislation in these matters.

The Scotland Act provides that relations with the European Communities (and their institutions) are reserved matters.[32] However, the Scotland Act does not reserve observing and implementing obligations under Community law. This same distribution of powers and obligations is found in the Northern Ireland Act. Relations with the European Communities are excepted matters but not observing and implementing Community obligations.[33] Thus European policy is to be a United Kingdom responsibility but the devolved legislatures have the authority and the obligation to implement and observe Community law. The obligation to observe Community law is spelled out very clearly in the legislation. It is outwith the legislative competence of either the Scottish Parliament or the Northern Ireland Assembly to enact any law that is incompatible with any Community obligation.[34] These provisions are essential to ensure that the United Kingdom complies with its Community obligations since the European Court of Justice has held that the Member State, as represented by its central government, is responsible for enforcing Community law in it territory.[35]

Powers delegated to Ministers of the Crown under the European Communities Act 1972 are transferred to Scottish Ministers in so far as they are within devolved competence.[36] One of the main implications of this transfer is that the Scottish Executive may make Scottish subordinate legislation to implement Community directives in areas falling under devolved competence such as the environment. The Scottish Executive may not exercise this power in such a way as to make subordinate legislation that is outside the legislative competence of the Scottish Parliament.[37] The Scottish Executive may not therefore make subordinate legislation that is contrary to Community law. To underline the importance of this provision, it is then explicitly stated in the Scotland Act that a member of the Scottish Executive has no power to make any subordinate legislation or do any other act that is incompatible with Community law.[38] In addition to these provisions, however, the Scotland Act also provides that despite this transfer of power to Scottish Ministers, the power to

---

[32] Scotland Act , Sched 5 para. 7(1).
[33] Northern Ireland Act, Sched 2 para. 3.
[34] Scotland Act s.29(2)(d), Northern Ireland Act s.6(2)(d).
[35] Case C–33/90 *Re Toxic Waste: Commission v. Italy* [1991] 1 E.C.R. 5987.
[36] Scotland Act s.53.
[37] Scotland Act s.54.
[38] Scotland Act s.57(2).

make subordinate legislation to implement a Community obligation remains with Ministers of the Crown.[39] Thus a concurrent power to implement Community law in Scotland is created. Both the Scottish Executive and United Kingdom government ministers have the power to make subordinate legislation for Scotland to implement Community law. Co-ordination is therefore essential to decide how United Kingdom obligations are to be observed. In particular, a decision must be made about who will exercise the power to make subordinate legislation in any particular case.

These same considerations apply in Northern Ireland where the obligation to implement Community law is not an excepted matter and is therefore transferred to Northern Ireland Ministers.[40] In exercising a transferred power, however, no Minister may confirm or approve any subordinate legislation, or do any other act, that is contrary to Community law.[41] Certain Community law matters fall into the Northern Irish category of reserved matters, for example, technical standards under Community law are reserved but not those relating to food or agricultural or fishery products.[42] Northern Ireland Ministers may thus only make subordinate legislation in these areas with the approval of the Secretary of State for Northern Ireland.

In Wales the legal position is slightly less complex since the National Assembly for Wales does not have legislative competence. The Government of Wales Act allows for the transfer of powers from Ministers of the Crown to the National Assembly for Wales for the purposes of implementing Community obligations in Wales[43]. Only limited powers under the European Communities Act have been transferred to the National Assembly for Wales under the Transfer Order.[44] Powers previously exercised by the Secretary of State for Wales are transferred to the National Assembly for Wales but there is no general transfer of powers to implement Community obligations. Where a power to make subordinate legislation has been transferred, it continues to be exercisable by a Minister of the Crown for the purposes of implementing Community obligations.[45] Thus again a

---

[39] Scotland Act s.57(1).
[40] Northern Ireland Act s.22.
[41] Northern Ireland Act s.24(1)(b).
[42] Northern Ireland Act Sched 3 para. 38.
[43] Government of Wales Act s.29.
[44] S.I. 1999/672 *The National Assembly for Wales (Transfer of Functions) Order.*
[45] Government of Wales Act Sched 3 para. 5.

concurrent power is created. In exercising these or any other powers the National Assembly for Wales must not act contrary to any Community law or obligation.[46]

The complexity of the division of powers between the devolved administrations and central government do require clear guide lines and clear lines of communication to ensure first that the devolved administrations are involved in formulating the policy that they will subsequently be required to implement and observe. They must also be given the opportunity to suggest a distinct regional approach to the implementation of Community obligations in their territory. There is nothing new in this since Community obligations in Northern Ireland and in Scotland have on many occasions been implemented by separate subordinate legislation. However, the central government has to be sure that Community obligations are complied with by the devolved administrations. If not, it would be the United Kingdom as a whole that would fall foul of Community law. In addition to all of these considerations, it may also prove to be more productive and efficient to have similar, if not the same, laws applying throughout the United Kingdom in respect of Community obligations. It may often be more efficient to adopt a United Kingdom line on questions of implementation of Community law.

The principles underlying intra-governmental relations on European Union matters are to be found in the Memorandum of Understanding.[47] Three principles are agreed:

- full involvement of the devolved administrations in the formulation of the United Kingdom's policy position

- mutual respect for the confidentiality of discussions

- adherence by all the devolved administrations to the resultant United Kingdom line.

These principles are expanded upon in the concordat on the co-ordination of E.U. policy published at the same time as the

---

[46] Government of Wales Act s.106(7).

[47] *Memorandum of Understanding and supplementary agreements* SE/99/36 laid before the Scottish Parliament by the Scottish Ministers October 1999. Part II contains the Supplementary Agreements including the Concordat on Co-ordination of European Union Policy Issues. This chapter is concerned only with this overarching Concordat. Separate Concordat do exist between departments, *e.g.* between the Scottish Executive and the DETR. Several of these Concordats also deal with European matters. They detail the specific obligations of both parties.

Memorandum of Understanding. Co-ordination of policy is required in two respects; in developing the United Kingdom position in negotiations and for implementing European obligations. The Concordat commits the United Kingdom government to involving the devolved administrations as directly and as fully in the development of European Union policies on matters coming within their devolved responsibility.[48] Participation in such consultations is subject to "mutual respect of the confidentiality of such discussions" and "adherence by the Scottish Executive to the resulting United Kingdom line . . . this line will reflect the interest of the United Kingdom as a whole".[49] Co-ordination mechanisms are intended to meet three objectives. First, they must ensure full and continuing involvement of all parties concerned including Ministers and officials. Thus participation and consultation is not intended to be a "one-off" exercise. Second, they must enable the United Kingdom to negotiate effectively and flexibly "in pursuit of a single United Kingdom policy line". Thus devolution is not intended to be allowed to dilute the strength of the United Kingdom position in negotiations in the Council of Ministers. Third, co-ordination mechanisms should ensure that European obligations are implemented "with consistency of effect and where appropriate timing". Exchange of information on new policy initiatives will also enable each administration to take such initiatives into consideration in formulating European Union policy.

These arrangements rely on a full exchange of information and the Concordats commit the United Kingdom government to provide the devolved administrations with "full and comprehensive information as early as possible" on European Union matters falling within devolved competence. In return the devolved administrations must respect the confidentiality of the information provided since "complete confidentiality is often essential in formulating a United Kingdom position . . . and in developing tactical responses".[50]

It is envisaged that consultation would normally take place on a bilateral basis between departments and most often by correspondence.[51] Consultation would therefore become a routine matter.

---

[48] Concordat on Co-ordination of European Union Policy Issues para. B1.3.
[49] Concordat on Co-ordination of European Union Policy Issues para. B1.4. Concordats in the same terms have been made between the Northern Ireland Executive and the Welsh Assembly Cabinet.
[50] Concordat on Co-ordination of European Union Policy Issues para. B3.2 and B3.3).
[51] Concordat on Co-ordination of European Union Policy Issues para. B3.6.

Where matters cannot be resolved bilaterally recourse to the Joint Ministerial Committee in European format will be necessary.[52] The Joint Ministerial Council would meet under the chair of the United Kingdom Foreign Minister and, failing agreement in this forum disputes would be referred to the Joint Ministerial Council Secretariat for resolution. A committee of senior officials supporting the Joint Ministerial Committee in European format has also been established to "make a major contribution to the resolution of E.U. issues".[53]

Ministers from the devolved administrations may also form part of the United Kingdom delegation to the Council of Ministers.[54] It is for the lead United Kingdom Minister to determine his/her team and to make the arrangements governing the extent of participation. The lead United Kingdom Minister retains overall responsibility for negotiations and the role of the devolved administrations is defined in terms of supporting and advancing the United Kingdom line.[55] In appropriate cases, a Minister from a devolved administration may speak for the United Kingdom in meetings of the Council of Ministers. When this happens they do so with the full weight of the United Kingdom behind them. Ministers from the Scottish Executive have attended meetings of the Environment Council and the Agriculture Council where matters have arisen touching on devolved responsibilities.

In terms of implementation, the key issue is again consultation. It is for the lead Whitehall department to inform the devolved administrations of European Union obligations.[56] The devolved administration, in consultation with the lead department, may decide to implement an obligation separately or opt for United Kingdom or Great Britain legislation.[57] Where a devolved administration decides to implement separately then again it has a duty to consult on its proposals to "produce consistency of effect and . . . timing". Co-ordination of all United Kingdom responses is undertaken by UKRep which retains its status as the Permanent representation in

---

[52] Concordat on Co-ordination of European Union Policy Issues para. B3.7.
[53] Concordat on Co-ordination of European Union Policy Issues para. B3.10.
[54] Concordat on Co-ordination of European Union Policy Issues para. B3.12.
[55] Concordat on Co-ordination of European Union Policy Issues para. B3.14.
[56] Concordat on Co-ordination of European Union Policy Issues para. B 3.16.
[57] Concordat on Co-ordination of European Union Policy Issues para. B3.17.

Brussels. UKRep assumes responsibility for informing the Commission of how Community obligations are implemented throughout the United Kingdom.[58]

Where infraction proceeding are brought against the United Kingdom, the Cabinet Office is responsible for co-ordinating the response.[59] If proceedings are brought as a result of an action or lack of action of one of the devolved administrations, that administration will draft the reply to the Commission.[60] If infraction proceedings continue and the matter is referred to the European Court of Justice, the devolved administration that is the cause of the proceedings will take the lead in preparation of the United Kingdom's submissions to the Court.[61] Any costs or penalties arising out of the failure of a devolved administration to comply with Community law must be met by that administration.[62]

The United Kingdom Permanent Representation in Brussels continues to represent the United Kingdom within the European Union.[63] However it is agreed that the devolved administrations may establish an office in Brussels to develop a link between other regional governments and with the Community institutions. Any such offices must act in a manner consistent with the responsibility of the United Kingdom Government for European matters.[64] The Scottish Executive opened an office in Brussels, Scotland House in 1999.

These mechanisms sit side by side with the Belfast Agreement institutions. Both the North/South Ministerial Council and the British-Irish Council have as part of their mandate the exchange of information on European Union matters and the possibility of developing common approaches to European Union matters.

What the totality of these arrangements show is that European policy co-ordination is firmly in the hands of the United Kingdom government. The lead department is always a Whitehall department. The Joint Ministerial Committee, in whatever format, is always chaired by a United Kingdom minister and disputes will be resolved within the United Kingdom Cabinet Office. Given the European dimension of so many devolved policy areas, the need to resist

---

[58] Concordat on Co-ordination of European Union Policy Issues para. B3.18.
[59] Concordat on Co-ordination of European Union Policy Issues para. B3.22.
[60] Concordat on Co-ordination of European Union Policy Issues para. B3.23.
[61] Concordat on Co-ordination of European Union Policy Issues para. B3.24.
[62] Concordat on Co-ordination of European Union Policy Issues para. B3.25.
[63] Concordat on Co-ordination of European Union Policy Issues para. B3.26.
[64] Concordat on Co-ordination of European Union Policy Issues para. B3.27.

"competence creep" is apparent. Policy co-ordination may prove to be a tendency towards policy imposition where powers are concurrent or shared. Under these circumstances, devolution would have occurred but not decentralisation.

It remains to be seen how robust the devolved administrations will prove to be in resisting encroachment from the centre. These arrangements are very new and they could not operate fully during the period of suspension of devolution in Northern Ireland. At this stage, it is impossible to draw firm conclusions as to whether genuine consultation will take place across the board and in all areas where consultation is both possible and desirable. This will be a matter for empirical research on a case by case basis.

Criticisms have been voiced over the use of Concordats. Bruce Crawford MSP, for example, described the concordat on European Union affairs as one of "the most polite gagging orders that we will ever see". He argued that the Memorandum of Understanding exposed "the control tendencies of the current United Kingdom government".[65]

The use of concordats has been criticised from several perspectives. Rawlings, for example, criticised the lack of a firm legal underpinning as well as the absence of any parliamentary supervision over them.[66] These fears were echoed in the debates in the Scottish Parliament and the National Assembly for Wales when the Memorandum of Understanding and the four overarching concordats were eventually published late in 1999.

Alex Neil MSP raised several concerns.[67] He accused the Scottish Executive of mistreating the Parliament by refusing to allow the Parliament any "opportunity to input its ideas" on the concordats. Furthermore, he criticised the lack of parliamentary scrutiny over the operation of the Joint Ministerial Committee. Minutes of the Joint Ministerial Council will not be available and Alex Neil asked "how can the Parliament scrutinise that work effectively if we do not have access to it". He added that it was beyond belief that minutes of the Bank of England's monetary policy committee could be made available but not those of the Joint Ministerial Committee. He also criticised the structure of the Joint Ministerial Committee, in

---

[65] Scottish Parliament Official Report October 7, 1999 col. 1133.
[66] R. Rawlings, "The New Model Wales" (1998) 4 *Journal of Law and Society* at 461.
[67] Scottish Parliament Official Report October 7, 1999 col 1113.

particular the fact that United Kingdom Ministers would simultaneously represent English and United Kingdom interests. He suggested that this meant that these interests are considered
synonymous. He proposed reform of the Joint Ministerial Committee by allowing a majority of the devolved administrations to
overrule the view of the English minister and that the convenership
be rotated amongst the four administrations.

Annabel Goldie MSP was equally concerned about the exclusion
of the Parliament from debating the terms of the concordats. In
response to a comment from Donald Dewar that internal administrative documents have not previously been debated by parliament she
pointed out that never before had there needed to be considerations
"of the regulation of relationships between two parliaments".[68]

In the National Assembly for Wales, Michael German AM raised
concerns about the secrecy and requirement of confidentiality that
runs through the Memorandum of Understanding. He argued that
this "was against the spirit of openness that we are trying to create in
this Assembly".[69]

Ron Davies, whilst broadly supportive of the concordats, was
concerned about some aspects of the handling of European business.
He noted that the Joint Ministerial Committee will reach agreements
rather than decisions and argued that this meant that decisions would
therefore be taken by the lead United Kingdom Minister who would
then seek to promote his/her colleagues in the Joint Ministerial
Committee of the benefits of that decision. If Ministers from the
devolved administrations do not agree, as he put it "tough, there is
no vote, the line is resolved by British Cabinet Ministers".[70] The
resultant United Kingdom line is then the one that binds ministers
from the devolved administrations. This inability to present a
specifically Welsh case in Europe was criticised by others in the
debate. Ieuan Wyn Jones, for example, would have preferred more
flexibility in this respect so as to allow the Assembly cabinet to
present a distinct Welsh case in Europe.[71]

The concordats are too new to be able to assess whether they are
indeed "gagging orders" or "the formal way for it [devolution] to
become a matter of administrative practice.[72] Taking the development

---

[68] Scottish Parliament Official Report October 7, 1999 col 1120.
[69] National Assembly for Wales Official Report October 7, 1999 at 31.
[70] National Assembly for Wales Official Report October 7, 1999 at 48.
[71] National Assembly for Wales Official Report October 7, 1999 at 57.
[72] National Assembly for Wales Official Report October 7, 1999 at 61 (Alun Michael).

of European policy as a case study it seems quite clear that central government retains overall control and intra-governmental relations are to be conducted under the auspices of rather than in partnership with the devolved administrations. It can be argued that this is the approach taken in the legislation and therefore there is nothing surprising in either the Memorandum of Understanding or in the Concordats. However, the problem does arise, and this is quite clear from the wording of the Concordats, that many of the areas of policy that have been devolved are areas which are governed by Community obligations. Under these circumstances there is always a possibility of competence creep where central government can use its powers in relation to European matters as a means of imposing a centrally determined policy on the devolved administrations. The intra-governmental mechanisms in themselves provide little reassurance against this possible encroachment on the powers of the devolved administrations. For these reasons the acceptance or adoption of a principle of subsidiarity or some other form of constitutional guarantee is needed to secure the devolution settlement. Otherwise intra-governmental mechanisms for policy co-ordination could become the back door to re-centralisation.

Chapter 6

Devolution issues

Writing in 1997, before the election of the Labour government but certainly in the hope that the election of that year would usher in a change of government committed to devolution in Scotland, Colin Boyd suggested some general principles for the review and resolution of disputes.[1] This chapter examines the mechanisms for the legal resolution of disputes under devolution in the light of Boyd's suggested principles. In particular, it attempts to measure whether the procedures and mechanisms provided for in the three devolution settlements line up to the general principles suggested by Boyd. His principles can be summarised as follows:

- a legal challenge should only be able to be mounted on questions relating to *vires* (competencies) or on the grounds that an action taken by a devolved institution conflicts with an international obligation entered into by the United Kingdom government

- disputes over competencies should be resolved by a judicial body

- all the parties to the dispute should have confidence in the judicial body

- the system chosen for the resolution of devolution disputes should be as speedy and efficient as possible.

Boyd takes the classical constitutional law line in adopting these principles. In particular by involving the judiciary in the resolution of

---

[1] C. Boyd, "Parliament and courts: Powers and Dispute Resolution" in T. StJ. N. Bates (ed.) *Devolution to Scotland: the Legal Aspects* (Edinburgh: T & T Clark, 1997).

devolution disputes there is an assumption that the judicial process is itself non-controversial and non-political. Constitutional courts are never neutral third parties in disputes but the use of a court system, as a system for the resolution of constitutional questions is well known. In one sense it is as good and may be better than the constant renegotiation of boundaries that might take place in the absence of such a court. Resort to judicial process at least creates a sense of stability in the constitutional order whilst allowing for movement within any political settlement.

In principle devolution disputes should arise infrequently if the control mechanisms in place within the devolved institutions work effectively. For example, pre-legislative scrutiny of both primary and delegated legislation should result in each institution acting within its own boundaries. Questions over the extent of competencies can also be resolved by informal means by way of discussion and liaison between law officers and the relevant government departments. The testing of the boundaries need not, therefore, result in the creation of a devolution issue that falls to be resolved by a judicial mechanism. It is only when these political mechanisms fail and a confusing legal situation becomes a dispute or when a direct challenge is made to an understanding of the limits of devolved competencies that the courts will become involved.

Definition of devolution issues

Boyd suggested that devolution issues should be limited to questions of competencies and potential breaches of United Kingdom international obligations. It is important therefore to see how devolution issues are defined. The approach taken in the legislation reflects the view that devolution issues should be defined narrowly.

The term "devolution issue" is one that is common to the Scotland Act,[2] the Government of Wales Act,[3] and the Northern Ireland Act.[4] Each Act defines the term in a slightly different way by listing the specific questions that are deemed to be devolution issues for the purposes of the Act. Perhaps one of the most succinct general

---

[2] Scotland Act s.98 and Sched. 6.
[3] Government of Wales Act s.109 and Sched. 8.
[4] Northern Ireland Act s.79 and Sched. 10.

definitions is the one given by Lord Hardie, the then Lord Advocate, in the debate on the Scotland Bill in the House of Lords. He stated that "devolution issues are essentially issues about the legislative competence of the Parliament and the devolved executive competence of the Scottish Executive".[5] Furthermore, he said that devolution issues are those that are "subject to special judicial procedures". Devolution issues can therefore be said to be those questions relating to the competence of the devolved institutions to act and the policing, ultimately by the Judicial Committee of the Privy Council, of the boundaries between the competencies of the devolved institutions and the United Kingdom government and parliament.

Issues relating to devolution may, however, arise in the course of other legal proceedings. During the debates in the House of Lords it was made clear that not all legal questions relating to devolution should be defined as devolution issues. In particular, it was said that procedural questions were not devolution issues. One example quoted by Lord Hardie was the potential challenge that "a Member of the Scottish Executive had made subordinate legislation without following the proper procedures". Lord Hardie stated that this would be a matter to be dealt with by "ordinary judicial review". In Scotland this means a judicial review brought in the Court of Session with appeal to the House of Lords.

To date, there have been only a couple of examples in the Scottish courts and none elsewhere. A judicial review was sought by the *Scotsman* newspaper of a decision by the Standards Committee of the Scottish Parliament to conduct hearings on the so-called lobbygate affair in private. The case was withdrawn following undertakings from the Presiding Officer. The hearings were subsequently held in public and all the Ministers named in the affair were exonerated.[6]

In the case brought against Lord Watson MSP, an action for interim interdict was refused by first the Lord Ordinary and then by the first Division of the Inner House of the Court of Session.[7] Lord Watson had been assisted by an anti-hunt lobby group in the preparation of his Protection of Wild Mammals Bill by which he sought to outlaw hunting with dogs in Scotland. The petitioners claimed that Lord Watson had acted in breach of article 6 of the 1999 Order regulating Members' interests which prohibits paid advocacy

---

[5] HL Deb vol 593 cols 583–584 October 8, 1998.
[6] Reported in *The Herald* October 5, 1999.
[7] *Whaley v. Lord Watson* 2000 SC 125.

on the part of any MSP.[8] The Lord Ordinary held that the court did not have jurisdiction to hear such a case or, if it did, it should not exercise its jurisdiction against a Member of the newly elected legislature. Furthermore, the Lord Ordinary held that section 40(3) of the Scotland Act, which prohibits any court from issuing an interdict against Parliament, and section 40(4) which prohibit a court from issuing an interdict against any MSP if the effect of such interdict is to give relief against the Parliament, were sufficient for him to hold that the court was not competent to issue the requested order.

The Inner House discussed the issue of jurisdiction and held that the Scottish Parliament was a creation of statute and was amenable to judicial review in the same way as other creations of statute such as local authorities. The mere fact that the Scottish Parliament was a Parliament did not take its actions out of the review of the courts. Admittedly, the court held, in exercising its legislative function, section 40 of the Scotland Act placed Parliament beyond the review of the courts but this did not mean that individual MSPs or officers of the Parliament were not subject to judicial control. However, the Inner House refused interdict on the ground that Lord Watson was not shown to be in breach of the Member's interests order.

This case makes clear, as Lord Hardie had earlier stated, that the Scottish Parliament, its Members and its officers are subject to the ordinary administrative law and procedures in respect of many of its functions. The Scottish Parliament is not sovereign, but subject to the rule of law administered by the courts in Scotland. Therefore, the courts may be faced with devolution issues in the narrow sense of the word defined in terms of competence. In addition, they may be faced with issues arising out of the devolution settlement. The former are to be dealt with under special procedures established by the relevant Act and the latter by the ordinary court procedures.

Six potential legal issues are defined in Schedule 6 of the Scotland Act as being devolution issues:

- whether an Act of the Scottish Parliament or a provision of such an Act is within the legislative competence of the Parliament
- whether any function, proposed or purported, is a function of the Scottish Ministers, the First Minister or the Lord Advocate

---

[8] S.I. 1999/1350 Scotland Act 1998 (Transitory and Transitional Provisions) (Members' Interests) Order 1999.

- whether a proposed or purported exercise of any function by a member of the Scottish Executive is, or would be, within devolved competence

- whether a purported or proposed exercise of any function by a member of the Scottish Executive is or would be incompatible with a Convention right or with Community law

- whether any failure to act on the part of any member of the Scottish Executive is similarly incompatible

- any other question about whether a function is exercisable within devolved competence or in or as regards Scotland and any other question arising about reserved matters.

The Government of Wales Act lists four potential devolution issues:

- whether a function is exercisable by the Assembly

- whether a purported or proposed exercise of a function by the Assembly is or would be within its powers

- whether the Assembly has failed to comply with a duty imposed on it

- whether the failure to act on the part of the Assembly is in contravention of one of the Convention rights.

The Northern Ireland Act lists four potential devolution issues

- whether any provision of an Act of the Assembly is within its legislative competence

- whether a proposed or purported exercise of a function by a Minister or Northern Ireland department would be invalid by virtue of section 24 (contravention of Community Law, Convention rights or principle of non discrimination on the ground of religious or political belief)

- whether a Minister or a Department had failed to comply with Community law or a Convention right or any order made by a Minister of the Crown to ensure compliance with any international obligation

- any question under the Act about excepted or reserved matters.

It is clear that the legislation limits devolution issues to questions of competence. In all three settlements, the type of question to be faced by the court is whether the relevant body has acted within its powers. These powers are defined in the devolution legislation. Furthermore, any exercise of a devolved power must not infringe a Convention right, as defined by the Human Rights Act 1998, nor must it infringe any Community law.

The courts are therefore faced with the difficulty of interpreting the devolution legislation alongside the Human Rights Act and any relevant Community legislation to determine whether a devolved body has acted within its powers. Some assistance is given to the courts as to the canons of interpretation to be applied. The Scotland Act states that where any provision of a Bill or Act of the Scottish Parliament or any Scottish subordinate legislation that could be read in such a way as to be outside competence should be read "as narrowly as is required for it to be within competence".[9] This allows the courts to exercise discretion in interpreting Scottish legislation so as to bring it, wherever possible, within the devolution settlement. A similar scheme operates under the Northern Ireland Act. Section 83 requires a reading of a provision "in the way which makes it within that competence".

A number of cases have arisen in the Scottish courts in relation to devolution issues. For example, the practice of appointing temporary sheriffs on annually renewable contracts was challenged in the Scottish courts as being incompatible with Article 6(1) of the European Convention on Human Rights—the right to a fair trial.[10] In this case the role of the Lord Advocate in bringing forward the names of suitable candidates for appointment and re-appointment as temporary sheriff was questioned given the Lord Advocate's role as head of the system of criminal prosecution in Scotland. The devolution issue in this case arose because the Lord Advocate is a member of the Scottish Executive and the exercise of any function by a member of the Scottish Executive must be compatible with Convention rights. The court held that the system of appointment of temporary sheriffs was a violation of the European Convention on

---

[9] Scotland Act s.101.
[10] *Hugh Starrs and another v. Procurator Fiscal, Linlithgow* [2000] SLT 42 and noted in A. O'Neill, "The European Convention and the Independence of the Scottish Judiciary" (2000) 63 *Modern Law Review* at 429.

Human Rights since the Convention required that judges be independent. Therefore in bringing prosecutions before temporary sheriffs, the Lord Advocate was acting ultra vires.[11]

The Scottish courts have also been asked to strike down an Act of the Scottish Parliament on the grounds that it infringes the European Convention on Human Rights. The Court of Session held that the Mental Health (Public Safety and Appeals) Act 1999, the first Act of the Scottish Parliament, was within the competence of the Scottish Parliament since it did not violate the European Convention on Human Rights.[12]

Devolution issues—the players

The three devolution settlements allocate responsibilities in respect of devolution issues to key legal personnel. A massive chess game has been created with specific rules on the moves that the various law officers can make. Each Act allocates particular functions to certain named law officers or other members of the executive. These functions can be defined in the following way:

- the right to initiate proceedings for the determination of a devolution issue

- the right to defend proceedings relating to a devolution issue

- the right to be notified of a devolution issue where such an issue arises in proceedings and subsequently to take part in the proceedings, as far as they relate to a devolution issue

- the right to require a court or tribunal to refer a devolution question to the Judicial Committee of the Privy Council.

---

[11] There have been a number of cases brought before the Scottish criminal courts challenging the system of criminal prosecutions or individual prosecutions in Scotland. For a discussion of these cases see C. Gane, *Devolution and Human Rights* and The Honourable Lord Reed, *Devolution and Human Rights* both papers presented to the conference "Legal Aspects of Devolution" at the Constitution Unit, September 23, 1999.

[12] *Anderson, Doherty and Reid v. The Scottish Ministers and the Advocate General for Scotland* the case was decided June 16, 2000. The opinion is reported on the Scottish Courts web site http://www.scotcourts.gov.uk/index1.htm.

The three Acts are written in slightly different terms to reflect the differences in the devolution settlements. The extent to which the devolved executives themselves may participate directly in proceedings is one such distinguishing feature. Whereas the Scotland Act stresses the importance of the role of the law officers, the Government of Wales Act introduces the Assembly itself as a potential party to the proceedings and the Northern Ireland Act envisages a role for the First Minister and deputy First Minister.

The tables below analyse the three relevant schedules to show the allocation of the four functions outlined above. All three acts specify that the allocation of functions within the Act is without prejudice to "any power to institute or defend proceedings exercisable by any other person". This means that a devolution issue might arise in the course of any proceedings in the courts in the United Kingdom. It is not only in proceedings raised by the law officers or, where relevant, the political institutions themselves, that devolution issues will emerge as part of the arguments of the parties.

Table 1. Right to initiate proceedings for the determination of a devolution issue

	Scotland Act— Schedule 6	GOWA— Schedule 8	NI Act— Schedule 10
In Scotland	Advocate General *or* Lord Advocate	Advocate General	Advocate General
In England and Wales	Attorney General	Attorney General	Attorney General
In Northern Ireland	Attorney General for Northern Ireland	Attorney General for Northern Ireland	Attorney General *or* Attorney General for Northern Ireland

Table 2. Right to defend proceedings

	Scotland Act— Schedule 6	GOWA— Schedule 8	NI Act— Schedule 10
In Scotland	Lord Advocate (where proceedings are commenced by Advocate General)	Not specified in Act	Advocate General *or* Attorney General for Northern Ireland *or* First Minister and Deputy First Minister acting jointly
In England and Wales	Lord Advocate	Not specified in Act	Attorney General *or* Attorney General for Northern Ireland *or* First Minister and deputy First Minister acting jointly
In Northern Ireland	Lord Advocate	Not specified in Act	Attorney General *or* Attorney General for Northern Ireland *or* First Minister and deputy First Minister acting jointly

Table 3. Right to be notified of a devolution issue in proceedings and thereafter participate

	Scotland Act— Schedule 6	GOWA— Schedule 8	NI Act— Schedule 10
In Scotland	Advocate General *and* Lord Advocate	Advocate General *and* Welsh Assembly	Advocate General *and* Attorney General for Northern Ireland *and* First Minister and deputy First Minister
In England and Wales	Attorney General *and* Lord Advocate	Attorney General *and* Welsh Assembly	Attorney General *and* Attorney General for Northern Ireland *and* First Minister and deputy First Minister
In Northern Ireland	Attorney General *and* Lord Advocate	Attorney General for Northern Ireland *and* Welsh Assembly	Attorney General *and* Attorney General for Northern Ireland *and* First Minister and deputy First Minister

151

Table 4. Right to order court to make referral to Judicial Committee

	Scotland Act—Schedule 6	GOWA—Schedule 8	NI Act-Schedule10
Right to order court to make referral to JCPC	Any of the following if party to the proceedings: Lord Advocate Advocate General Attorney General Attorney General for Northern Ireland	Relevant Law Officer (not named in Act but presumably any of the following if party to the proceedings) Advocate General Attorney General Attorney General for Northern Ireland *or* Welsh Assembly	Any of the following if party to the proceedings: Attorney General Attorney General for Northern Ireland First Minister and deputy First Minister acting jointly Advocate General

It is possible to make some sense of this seemingly confusing pattern of potential proceedings and roles by examining the roles of the various legal actors and by analysing the types of proceedings in which devolution issues can be raised. It is important to note the absence of a role for the Scottish Parliament and the Northern Ireland Assembly in devolution proceedings. Neither of the relevant Acts envisages a specific role for these parliamentary bodies in the protection of the devolution settlement. That function is taken over by the executive branch of government. The Welsh Assembly, which does have a role in devolution cases, is not a parliamentary body. Devolution in Wales is executive devolution and the Welsh Assembly collectively exercises executive powers.

The law officers have a major role to play in the resolution of devolution disputes in the courts. However, no exact comparison can be drawn between the roles of the various law officers. The devolution settlements were bolted on to pre-existing legal institutions. The offices of Lord Advocate and Attorney General had developed in their own ways to serve specific purposes. Devolution adds a further, and perhaps confusing, dimension to these institutions. This can be seen in the examination of the roles and functions of the law officers outlined below. Powers have been transferred to two law officers, both of whom had originally been members of the United Kingdom executive, the Lord Advocate and the Attorney General. The Advocate General for Scotland is a newly created post specifically to deal with the gap that the transfer had created. The seemingly anomalous position of the Northern Irish First Minister and Deputy First Minister is explicable because of the absence of a law officer in the Northern Ireland settlement. There is no law officer within the Northern Ireland executive. The post of Attorney General for Northern Ireland is recognised in the legislation but this post would be one within the United Kingdom government. Political sensitivities preclude the creation of a Northern Ireland law officer as such yet there does appear to be a clear need for a recognised law officer of some sort within each of the devolved administrations. The Government of Wales Act does not create any law officer for Wales but the National Assembly for Wales has felt the need to create a new post, Counsel General for Wales.

The Lord Advocate

The office of the Lord Advocate has been known in Scotland since 1483.[13] In more recent times the Lord Advocate has been one of the law officers of the United Kingdom government. Prior to devolution, he was responsible for advising the United Kingdom government on matters relating to Scots law and was accountable to the United Kingdom parliament for the operation of the criminal justice system in Scotland. The Lord Advocate was a Minister of the Crown. According to Brazier appointees to the post did not always come from within the ranks of parliament but a convention had developed since 1969 that the Lord Advocate would be awarded a life peerage

---

[13] Lord Hardie in evidence to Justice and Home Affairs Committee, Justice and Home Affairs Committee Official Report, August 31, 1999 col. 39.

should he/she not be a Member of the House of Commons.[14] Like his/her English counterpart, the Attorney General, the Lord Advocate was not normally a member of the Cabinet but could attend, at the request of the Cabinet, to discuss specific issues.[15]

The Scotland Act provides that the Lord Advocate shall be a member of the Scottish Executive, collectively known as the Scottish Ministers.[16] As no person can hold a post simultaneously as a Minister of the Crown and as a Scottish Minister, the position of the Lord Advocate as a Minister of the Crown thereby ceases. The post is therefore devolved. The Lord Advocate continues to be a political appointee—recommended to her Majesty by the First Minister after seeking agreement of the Scottish Parliament.[17] The Lord Advocate retains his/her post as the head of the system of criminal prosecution in Scotland and, in this capacity, must act "independently of any other person".[18]

The Lord Advocate need not be a Member of the Scottish Parliament but where he/she is not arrangements are made to allow the Lord Advocate to participate in proceedings without a vote.[19] Lord Hardie, who was Lord Advocate prior to devolution and continued in that role after devolution, was not an MSP but is a life peer and is therefore a Member of the House of Lords. His successor, Colin Boyd, is neither an MSP nor a peer.

Lord Hardie attempted to clarify his role after devolution to the members of the Justice and Home Affairs Committee of the Scottish Parliament.[20] In a statement to the committee, he listed five major functions of the Lord Advocate after devolution:

- to provide legal advice to the Scottish Executive particularly on questions of competence and of compatibility of proposed policies or legislation with the European Convention and European Community law

- to take a view on whether the provisions of a Bill are within the competence of the Scottish Parliament and, where necessary, to

---

[14] R. Brazier, *Constitutional Practice* (Oxford: Clarendon Press, 1995) 55.

[15] A.W. Bradley and K.D. Ewing, *Constitutional and Administrative Law* (12th ed.) (London: Longman, 1977) at 291.

[16] Scotland Act s.44.

[17] Scotland Act s.48.

[18] Scotland Act s.48(5).

[19] Scotland Act s.27.

[20] Justice and Home Affairs Committee Official Report, August 31, 1999 col. 39.

refer Bills to the Judicial Committee of the Privy Council on questions of competence and to raise and defend proceedings in relation to devolution issues in other courts

- to liaise with the English law officers on legal questions relating to devolution issues (he did not mention liaison with the Attorney General for Northern Ireland)

- to take responsibility for the office of Solicitor to the Scottish Executive

- to exercise retained functions in respect of the duty of prosecution in the public interest, as head of the system of prosecutions and investigations of deaths in Scotland and as head of the prosecuting authority for Scotland: the Crown Office and the Procurator Fiscal service.

The first four of these functions can clearly be defined in terms of a constitutional role as part of the process of devolution whereas the last relates to the operation of a devolved area, the system of prosecution. Irrespective of the integrity of the person holding the post of Lord Advocate, there is clearly a confusion of roles here which has little to do with traditional separation of powers arguments. The first Lord Advocate was a member of the United Kingdom legislature. However, his successor has not been given a life peerage. The constitutional convention that the Lord Advocate, if he/she were not an MP, would be awarded a life peerage seems therefore to have been discontinued as it no longer serves a useful purpose (subject to whatever emerges as reform of the House of Lords). The Lord Advocate is currently a Minister within the Scottish Cabinet. In the determination of policy, for example in the definition of statutory criminal offences, he/she will advise and participate in decision making. In this respect the Lord Advocate is bound by collective ministerial responsibility. The Lord Advocate is not, however, bound by collective ministerial responsibility in matters relating to the operation of the criminal justice system in terms of investigation and prosecution of crimes. He/she is required to operate without regard to any political influence in this respect.[21] Bradley and Ewing have commented that in the English context "it is regarded as preferable that he (the Attorney General who has a

---

[21] s.48(5) Scotland Act requires the Lord Advocate to continue to take such decisions "independently of any other person".

similar role in respect of prosecutions) should remain outside the Cabinet as the government's chief legal adviser, attending particular Cabinet meetings only when summoned".[22] Lord Hardie's response to these types of arguments was to say that in the past Lord Advocates had attended and played a part in cabinet committees and their independence had not suffered. Such a statement is, of course, unverifiable. The principle still remains that there is a potential conflict of interest between the policy making and the policy implementation roles on vital questions in the operation of the legal system. The third issue is one of accountability. Despite being a member of the Scottish Cabinet, the Lord Advocate is not required to be a member of the legislature. He/she is therefore accountable to a body of which he/she in not an elected member. It was precisely because the Lord Advocate was not always appointed from amongst the ranks of MPs that the convention developed that he/she would become a Member of the House of Lords to participate in the proceedings and to answer questions about the operation of the prosecution service. Ministerial accountability has, in the United Kingdom context, been seen in this direct participation of ministers in one or other of the Houses of Parliament. It may be argued that section 27 of the Scotland Act that enables the Law Officers to participate in proceedings without having a vote is sufficient to create the accountability of the Lord Advocate to the Scottish Parliament. Lord Hardie participated in debates and answered questions but, in doing so, he was criticised for being too political and appearing as a government spokesperson.

There is obviously a fine line to be drawn here between what is a political/constitutional/legal role and one that is a more purely legal role. The Scotland Act in determining that the Lord Advocate would be a member of the Scottish Executive has created difficulties. The cases discussed above in relation to the independence of the Scottish judiciary have demonstrated in a very radical way the need to separate out the functions of the Scottish Law officers and to separate his/her legal and political roles. The decision to create a Minister of Justice and a Justice and Home Affairs Committee of the Scottish Parliament, decisions taken after the devolution legislation was enacted, have undermined the need for the Lord Advocate to have a political role and there is a strong argument now for amendment of the legislation.

---

[22] A.W. Bradley and K.D. Ewing, in note 15, at 444.

The Lord Advocate is a key player in the determination of devolution issues under the Scotland Act. The Lord Advocate may refer a question as to the competence of the Scottish Parliament to enact a Bill to the Judicial Committee.[23] He/she may also institute proceedings for the determination of a devolution issue in the Scottish courts and defend any such proceedings where they are brought by the Advocate General for Scotland.[24] He/she may defend proceedings brought under the Scotland Act by the Attorney General in the courts in England and Wales or by the Attorney General for Northern Ireland in courts in Northern Ireland.[25] Where a devolution issue is raised under the Scotland Act in a court or tribunal in Scotland, the Lord Advocate has the right to be notified of the issue and thereafter has the right to participate in proceedings.[26] He/she is given a similar right in proceedings under the Scotland Act in courts in England and Wales and in Northern Ireland.[27] Finally, the Lord Advocate may require a court or tribunal in any proceedings in which he/she is a party to refer a devolution issue to the Judicial Committee.[28]

The Solicitor General for Scotland

Like the Lord Advocate, the Solicitor General for Scotland was, prior to devolution, a law officer of the United Kingdom government. Brazier states that from 1974-1987 the Solicitor General was chosen from amongst the ranks of MPs. It was when Peter Fraser lost his seat in the 1987 election that this convention was discontinued.[29] The Solicitor General prior to devolution, Colin Boyd, was not an MP. The post of Solicitor General was devolved by virtue of the Scotland Act.[30] The Solicitor General is now a law officer of the Scottish Executive. He/she is the junior minister working with the senior law officer. The Solicitor General need not be an MSP. He/she may

---

[23] Scotland Act s.33.
[24] Scotland Act, Sched. 6, Pt II, para. 4(1).
[25] Scotland Act, Sched. 6, Pt III, para. 15(2) and Pt IV, para. 25(2).
[26] Scotland Act, Sched. 6, Pt II, paras 5 and 6.
[27] Scotland Act, Sched. 6 Pt III, paras 16 and 17 and Part IV paras 26 and 27.
[28] Scotland Act Sched. 6, Part V, para. 33.
[29] Brazier in note 14 above.
[30] Scotland Act s.44.

participate in proceedings of the Scottish Parliament on the same terms as the Lord Advocate.[31] The Solicitor General is given no specific functions in dealing with devolution issues.

The Advocate General for Scotland

The transfer of the Lord Advocate and the Solicitor General to the Scottish Executive would have resulted in the United Kingdom government being deprived of any direct access to advice on Scottish legal matters. It would have also have deprived Westminster of the opportunity to call the government to account on reserved matters as they apply in Scotland and in so far as they are legal questions. The solution was to create a new post, the Advocate General for Scotland. Section 87 of the Scotland Act creates the post of Advocate General for Scotland by amending the House of Commons Disqualification Act and the Ministerial and Other Salaries Act. This has the effect of creating a new ministerial post in the United Kingdom government. The Advocate General for Scotland is, therefore, accountable to the Westminster Parliament.

The first Advocate General for Scotland, Lynda Clark, is a member of the House of Commons. She represents a Scottish seat. Future appointees will presumably either be drawn from the House of Commons or, as was the case with the Lord Advocate in more recent times, be appointed to the House of Lords if he/she is not an M.P.

The Advocate General for Scotland is now the Law Officer who is responsible for giving advice on matters relating to Scots Law to the United Kingdom government. The Advocate General is responsible for the Solicitor to the Advocate General for Scotland, who has taken over the functions of the Scottish Office Solicitors in their role of providing advice on Scottish legal matters to United Kingdom government departments. He/she is given statutory duties under the Scotland Act, including the power to refer Scottish Bills to the Judicial Committee to determine whether they are within the powers of the Scottish Parliament.[32] The Advocate General for Scotland may also initiate proceedings for the determination of a devolution issue under the Scotland Act in Scottish courts[33] or for the determination

---

[31] Scotland Act s.27.
[32] Scotland Act s.33(1).
[33] Scotland Act Sched. 6, Part II, para. 4.

of a devolution issue under the Government of Wales Act in the Scottish courts.[34] When a devolution issue under the Scotland Act arises in a Scottish court or where a devolution issue under the Government of Wales Act arises in a Scottish court, the Advocate General for Scotland has the right to be notified of the issue and thereafter has the right to participate in the proceedings.[35] The Advocate General intervened for the first time in a case where the legality of the first Act of the Scottish Parliament, the Mental Health Public Safety and Appeals Scotland Act, was challenged.[36] Where the Advocate General for Scotland is a party to proceedings under the Scotland Act, the Government of Wales Act or the Northern Ireland Assembly, he/she may require the court to refer a devolution issue for determination to the Judicial Committee.[37]

Attorney General

The Attorney General is the senior English Law Officer. He/she is also the senior Welsh law officer given the assimilation of the English and Welsh legal systems. Bradley and Ewing state that the Attorney General is "invariably" a member of the House of Commons,[38] although, according to Brazier, parliamentary questions on legal matters are now taken by the Parliamentary Secretary to the Lord Chancellor's Department. The Attorney General is a Minister in the United Kingdom Government but is not normally a member of the Cabinet. As stated above, his/her membership of the Cabinet has been thought undesirable because of the responsibility of the Attorney General in relation to criminal prosecutions.

The Attorney General has a role to play in the three devolution settlements. He/she may refer a question on the competence of the Scottish Parliament to enact a Bill to the Judicial Committee as part of the post legislative scrutiny procedures.[39] He/she may also institute

---

[34] Government of Wales Act, Sched. 8, Pt III, para. 13(1).
[35] Scotland Act Sched. 6, Pt II, paras 5 and 6 and Government of Wales Act, Sched. 8, Pt III para. 14.
[36] See note 12.
[37] Scotland Act Sched. 6, Pt V para. 33, Government of Wales Act Sched. 8, Pt V para. 30, Northern Ireland Act, Sched. 10, Pt V, para. 33.
[38] A.W. Bradley and K.D. Ewing in note 15, at 291.
[39] Scotland Act s.33(1).

proceedings for the determination of a devolution issue under the Scotland Act in courts in England and Wales[40] or in proceedings under the Northern Ireland Act in courts in Northern Ireland[41] or in proceedings arising under the Government of Wales Act in courts in England and Wales.[42] The Attorney General may also defend devolution proceedings brought under the Northern Ireland Act in courts in Northern Ireland.[43] The Scotland Act gives the Attorney General the right to be notified of a devolution issue arising in the courts in England and Wales and thereafter to participate in such proceedings.[44] He/she has similar rights in relation to devolution issues arising under the Northern Ireland Assembly in courts in Northern Ireland and to devolution issues arising under the Government of Wales Act in courts in England and Wales.[45] Where the Attorney General is a party to proceedings under the Scotland Act, the Government of Wales Act or the Northern Ireland Assembly, he/she may require the court to refer a devolution issue for determination to the Judicial Committee.[46]

The Attorney General for Northern Ireland

At the time of writing there is no separate post of Attorney General for Northern Ireland. A separate post of Attorney General for Northern Ireland did exist during the Stormont era. The Attorney General for Northern Ireland was always a member of the House of Commons and provided advice to the government on Northern Irish matters.[47] After the demise of Stormont the post was integrated into the post of Attorney General so that now the Attorney General for England and Wales acts for Northern Ireland as well. The Northern Ireland Act does not create a post for a law officer in the Northern

---

[40] Scotland Act Sched. 6, Part III, para. 15(1).
[41] Northern Ireland Act, Sched. 10, Pt II para. 4(1).
[42] Government of Wales Act, Sched. 8, Pt II, para. 4(1) .
[43] Northern Ireland Act, Sched. 10, Pt II, para. 4(1).
[44] Scotland Act Sched. 6 Pt III paras 16 and 17.
[45] Northern Ireland Act Sched. 10, paras 5 and 6 and Government of Wales Act Sched. 8, Pt II, para. 5.
[46] Scotland Act Sched. 6, Pt V para. 33, Government of Wales Act Sched. 8, Pt V para. 30, Northern Ireland Act, Sched. 10, Pt V, para. 33.
[47] B. Dickson, *The Legal System of Northern Ireland* ((Belfast: SLS Legal Publications, 1984) at 12.

Ireland Executive comparable to the Lord Advocate in Scotland or the Attorney General in England and Wales.

However, there is a distinction drawn in the Northern Ireland Act between the Attorney General and the Attorney General for Northern Ireland. The latter is given the right (shared with others) to initiate proceedings in the Northern Irish courts and to defend such proceedings. He/she also may refer cases to the Judicial Committee. The Attorney General for Northern Ireland will not be a member of the Northern Ireland Executive, he/she will continue to be a law officer in the United Kingdom government and legal advice will continue to be provided from London.

The Attorney General for Northern Ireland may refer a question on the legislative competence of the Northern Ireland Assembly to enact a provision of a Bill or a Bill to the Judicial Committee as part of the post-legislative scrutiny arrangements for the Northern Ireland Assembly.[48] He/she may also institute proceedings in the courts in Northern Ireland for the determination of a devolution dispute arising under the Northern Ireland Act,[49] or for the determination of a devolution issue arising under the Scotland Act in the courts in Northern Ireland[50] or for a determination of a devolution issue under the Government of Wales Act in these courts.[51] The Attorney General for Northern Ireland has the right to be notified of a devolution issue arising in the courts in Northern Ireland and thereafter as the right to participate in matters under the Scotland Act,[52] in matters arising under the Northern Ireland Act[53] or in matters under the Government of Wales Act.[54] Where the Attorney General for Northern Ireland is a party to proceedings under the Scotland Act, the Government of Wales Act or the Northern Ireland Assembly, he/she may require the court to refer a devolution issue for determination to the Judicial Committee.[55]

---

[48] Northern Ireland Act s.11.
[49] Northern Ireland Act Sched. 10, Pt II, para. 4(1).
[50] Scotland Act, Sched. 6, Pt IV, para. 25.
[51] Government of Wales Act, Sched. 8, Pt IV, para. 23(1).
[52] Scotland Act, Sched. 6, Pt IV, paras 26 and 27.
[53] Northern Ireland Act Sched. 10, Part II, paras 5 and 6.
[54] Government of Wales Act, Sched. 8, Pt IV, para. 24(1).
[55] Scotland Act Sched. 6, Pt V para. 33, Government of Wales Act Sched. 8, Pt V para. 30, Northern Ireland Act, Sched. 10, Pt V, para. 33.

First Minister and Deputy First Minister (Northern Ireland)

In the absence of a specified law officer for Northern Ireland, the First Minister and Deputy First Minister have a role to play in the judicial resolution of devolution issues. The right to defend proceedings arising in the Northern Ireland courts under the Northern Ireland Act is given to the First Minister and Deputy First Minister.[56] Under the Scottish settlement this role is given to the Lord Advocate who is a member of the Scottish Executive. The First Minister and Deputy First Minister also have a right to be notified of a devolution issue arising under the Northern Ireland Assembly and the right to participate in such proceedings thereafter.[57] Again this is a role given to the Lord Advocate in the Scottish settlement. Unlike the Lord Advocate, the First Minister and Deputy First Minister do not have the right to participate in court proceedings outside Northern Ireland. This role is given to the Attorney General for Northern Ireland. The First Minister and Deputy First Minister may require a court in which they are party to proceedings to refer a devolution issue to the Judicial Committee.[58]

Counsel General to the National Assembly for Wales

The Government of Wales Act does not provide for the creation of any new law officers. Indeed the only law officer mentioned in the Act is the Attorney General. Rawlings reports that the White Paper had "signalled reliance on the law officers in London."[59] However, the Assembly is given a role in the judicial resolution of devolution issues. It has the right to be notified of a devolution issue arising under the Government of Wales Act in courts in England and Wales,[60] in courts in Scotland[61] or in courts in Northern Ireland.[62] In addition it may require that a case be referred to the Judicial Committee if it is a party to the proceedings.[63]

---

[56] Northern Ireland Act Sched. 10, Part II, para. 4(2).
[57] Northern Ireland Act Sched. 10, Part II, para. 5.
[58] Northern Ireland Act Sched. 10, Part IV, para. 33.
[59] R. Rawlings, "Living with the lawyers" *Agenda* (Summer 1999) at 32.
[60] Government of Wales Act, Sched. 8, Pt II, para. 5(1).
[61] Government of Wales Act, Sched. 8, Pt III, para. 14(1).
[62] Government of Wales Act, Sched. 8, Pt IV, para. 24(1).
[63] Government of Wales Act Sched. 8, Pt V, para. 30.

The post of Counsel General to the National Assembly for Wales has therefore been created to advise and represent the Assembly. Unlike the law officers discussed above, the Counsel General for Wales is not a political appointment. It is a post created within the civil service. This is why the first Counsel General, Winston Roddick, has described the post as being "unique". The Counsel General for Wales is a new type of law officer. Independent of party politics and appointed through civil service procedures, the Counsel General is appointed on the basis of legal expertise and merit. His/her function is "to give authoritative advice on matters of law".[64] Of course there are lawyers already working within the civil service and within the civil services of the devolved administrations. The legal secretariat within the Scottish Parliament and the Office of the Solicitor to the Scottish Executive, for example, are staffed with lawyers working within the civil service. Indeed there are civil service lawyers providing legal advice for the Office of the Assembly.

The office of Counsel General for Wales appears to be a hybrid between the roles of these civil service based lawyers and a traditional, politically appointed, law officer. "The sudden emergence" of the post is, according again to Rawlings, the best illustration of "the role for law involved in devolution, as also the ad hoc piecemeal character of the institutional developments". The Counsel General is intended to be a high profile legal figure but not a high profile political one. This profile will be developed by the participation of the Counsel General on the part of the Assembly in devolution proceedings. If devolution is to develop and expand in Wales, however, it may be necessary to create new legal posts in Wales corresponding to the Lord Advocate or a Welsh Attorney General.

The Legal Actors

The lack of symmetry in these arrangements is not fatal, it is merely extremely confusing. The choice of the legal actors whose functions are described above as participants in cases where devolution issues are at issue is explicable only in an historical context. There is no logical pattern corresponding to an overall vision of how constitutional issues can be resolved in the courts. Legal responsibilities in

---

[64] W. Roddick, *The Legal Challenges Facing Wales,* paper presented to the conference on Legal Aspects of Devolution, September 23, 1999, Constitution Unit, London.

relation to devolution have been bolted on to the existing functions of the Lord Advocate and the Attorney General. Both of these represent the executive branch of government in Scotland (the Lord Advocate) and England, Wales and Northern Ireland (the Attorney General). Two new posts have been created. The Advocate General for Scotland is a law officer for the United Kingdom government. The Counsel General for Wales is a civil service based law officer for the Welsh Assembly. Questions relating to the need for a law officer in Northern Ireland have been avoided as being too politically sensitive. In these circumstances the Northern Ireland Act treats the First Minister and the Deputy First Minister as if they were law officers.

Devolution could have provided the opportunity to rethink the role of the law officers in government and in the constitution and perhaps to harmonise these roles across the United Kingdom. Certainly in Scotland, where there is now a Minister for Justice for the first time, there is not a strong argument for having the Lord Advocate within the Scottish cabinet. Political responsibility for the operation of the legal system in Scotland is in the hands of the Minister for Justice who is an MSP. Furthermore, it is perfectly feasible, as the Welsh case demonstrates, for legal advice to be provided to the executive from within the civil service or, as is the case in Northern Ireland, from sources independent of the state.

Procedures

The procedures for dealing with devolution issues are set out in the relevant schedules of the devolution legislation. The same scheme of procedures applies to devolution issues whether they arise in relation to the Scotland Act, the Government of Wales Act or the Northern Ireland Act.

Two different types of legal actions are envisaged: references and appeals. Where a devolution issue arises in a lower court or in a tribunal, that court or tribunal may and some tribunals must refer the matter to a higher court within that jurisdiction. The court making the reference stays its proceedings until the devolution issue has been settled. There is a clear analogy here with the procedure for a preliminary ruling to the European Court of Justice under Article 234 TEC. An appeal, by contrast, leads to the higher court giving judgment on the matter and overturning or upholding the decision of the lower court.

Proceedings in Scotland

(A) CIVIL PROCEEDINGS

It is mandatory that a tribunal from which there is no appeal should refer a devolution issue to the Inner House of the Court of Session.[65] Any other tribunal may refer the matter to the Inner House.[66] A lower Scottish court may make such a reference.[67] A lower court would include the Sheriff Court, including appeals heard by the Sheriff Principal, and the Outer House of the Court of Session. In these cases, the Inner House must decide the devolution issue. However, if a devolution issue arises in proceedings in the Inner House, it may refer a devolution issue to the Judicial Committee of the Privy Council.[68]

Appeal lies to the Judicial Committee against the determination of a devolution issue of the Inner House, where that issue has been raised in a reference to the Inner House from a lower court or a tribunal.[69] No leave to appeal is necessary in these cases. Leave to appeal to the Judicial Committee is required in those civil cases where there is no appeal from the Inner House to the House of Lords. The Inner House determines whether leave to appeal may be granted although special leave may be granted by the Judicial Committee itself.[70]

The Act of Sederunt (Devolution Issues Rules) 1999 regulates the procedures of the Court of Session where devolution issues arise in proceedings under the devolution legislation.[71] Unless the Court, on cause shown, determines otherwise a devolution issue must be raised before evidence is led. The party raising the issue must specify the facts and circumstances and contentions of law in sufficient detail to

---

[65] Scotland Act 1998 Sched. 6, Pt II, para. 8, Government of Wales Act Sched. 8, Pt III para. 16, Northern Ireland Act Sched. 10, Part IV, para. 26.

[66] Scotland Act 1998 Sched. 6, Part II, para. 8, Government of Wales Act Sched. 8, Part III para. 16, Northern Ireland Act Sched. 10, Part IV, para. 26.

[67] Scotland Act 1998 Sched. 6, Part II, para. 7, Government of Wales Act Sched. 8, Part III para. 15, Northern Ireland Act Sched. 10, Part IV, para. 25.

[68] Scotland Act 1998 Sched. 6, Part II, para. 10, Government of Wales Act Sched. 8, Part III para. 18, Northern Ireland Act Sched. 10, Part IV, para. 28.

[69] Scotland Act 1998 Sched. 6, Part II, para. 12, Government of Wales Act Sched. 8, Part III para. 20, Northern Ireland Act Sched. 10, Part IV, para. 30.

[70] Scotland Act 1998 Sched. 6, Part II, para. 13, Government of Wales Act Sched. 8, Part III para. 21, Northern Ireland Act Sched. 10, Part IV, para. 31.

[71] S.I. 1999/1345 (S.100).

enable the Court to determine whether a devolution issue has actually arisen. Intimation of a devolution issue to the relevant law officer (the Lord Advocate and the Advocate General) can either be done by the service of a writ on the relevant authority or in any other case, the party raising the issue must crave a warrant from the court to intimate the issue to the relevant authority. The Court will order intimation where it appears that a devolution issue does in fact arise. The relevant authority then has fourteen days to specify his/her intention to take part as a party in proceedings. His/her minute of submissions must be lodged within a further seven days.

Civil proceedings in the Sheriff Court are also governed by Act of Sederunt.[72] The same pattern of rules emerges with a requirement that a devolution issue cannot be raised after proof has commenced unless the Sheriff, on cause shown, otherwise determines. One difference in the procedure is that the initiating document must also include a crave for a warrant to intimate a devolution issue to the relevant authority. The Sheriff Court must grant an order of intimation. If a devolution issue is raised subsequently the Sheriff will issue an order of intimation if it appears to him/her that a devolution issue arises. The relevant authority is given fourteen days in which to enter an appearance as a party and must lodge a note of his/her written submissions within a further seven days.

References to the Judicial Committee are governed by the Judicial Committee (Devolution Issues) Rules Order 1999.[73] These rules specify that the reference shall set out:

- the question referred
- the address of the parties
- name and address of persons who applied for or required the reference to be made
- a concise statement of the background to the case including the facts of the case and the main issues and contentions of the parties
- the relevant law
- the reasons why an answer to the question is necessary for the purpose of disposing of the proceedings.[74]

---

[72] S.I. 1999/1347.

[73] S.I. 1999/665.

[74] This is not a requirement found in the Scotland Act. However, it is a similar rule to that provided in the Act of Sederunt governing references to the European Court of Justice. S.I. 1999/1281 Rules of the Court.

Judgments already given in the proceedings must be annexed to the request for a reference.

Where the Sheriff Court makes a reference either to the Court of Session (which then must determine the issue) or directly to the Judicial Committee it must supply the same information as is required of the Court of Session in a reference to the Judicial Committee.[75] The Sheriff Court would normally refer a devolution issue to the Inner House but the Lord Advocate or the Advocate General may require the Sheriff Court to refer the matter to the Judicial Committee, in preference to the Court of Session, if he/she is a party in the proceedings.

(B) CRIMINAL PROCEEDINGS

Where a devolution issue arises in the course of criminal proceedings a lower criminal court may refer the devolution issue to the High Court of Justiciary.[76] In its turn the High Court of Justiciary may refer a devolution matter to the Judicial Committee.[77] It may not make such a reference where a lower court has referred the devolution issue to it.[78]

An appeal against the determination of a devolution issue by the High Court of Justiciary, whether on a reference from a lower court or not, lies to the Judicial Committee. Leave to appeal from the High Court is necessary but special leave may be granted by the Judicial Committee.[79]

The Act of Adjournal (Devolution Issues) Rules 1999[80] governs criminal proceedings in the High Court of Justiciary and the Sheriff Court. Proceedings on indictment are governed by Rule 40.2 which provides that a party proposing to raise a devolution issue must notify the intention to do so within seven days of service of the indictment. The Notice is served by the Clerk on other parties and the relevant

---

[75] S.I. 1999/1347 Sched. 2.

[76] Scotland Act 1998 Sched. 6, Part II, para. 9, Government of Wales Act Sched. 8, Part III para. 17, Northern Ireland Act Sched. 10, Part IV, para. 27.

[77] Scotland Act 1998 Sched. 6, Part II, para. 11, Government of Wales Act Sched. 8, Part III para. 19, Northern Ireland Act Sched. 10, Part IV, para. 29.

[78] Scotland Act 1998 Sched. 6, Part II, paras 9 and 11, Government of Wales Act Sched. 8, Part III paras 17 and 19, Northern Ireland Act Sched. 10, Part IV, paras 27 and 29.

[79] Scotland Act 1998 Sched. 6, Part II, para. 13, Government of Wales Act Sched. 8, Part III para. 21, Northern Ireland Act Sched. 10, Part IV, para. 31.

[80] S.I. 1999/1346.

authority.[81] The relevant authority must give notice of his/her intention to take part in proceedings as a party within seven days. That notice is then copied to the other parties and to the Lord Advocate where he/she is not already a party. In summary proceedings a party must give notice of his/her intention to raise a devolution issue before the accused, or where there is more than one accused, any accused is called upon to plead. As in the High Court the Clerk notifies the other parties including the relevant authority that a devolution issue has been raised and the relevant authority may then take part in proceedings. No party can raise a devolution issue except in accordance with these rules unless the court, on cause shown, determines otherwise. The party raising the issue must specify the facts and circumstances and contentions of law in sufficient detail to allow the court to determine whether a devolution issue does in fact arise.

When a lower court refers a devolution issue to the High Court of Justiciary, it must make an order giving directions to the parties and give reasons for making the reference. If a devolution issue is raised in the course of proceedings, however, the court in which the issue is raised must decide the issue itself and not make a referral. A court may also refer the issue to the Judicial Committee and, if it does so must provide the details required in Rule 2.9 of the Rules of the Judicial Committee (Devolution Issues) described above.

The Act of Adjournal has been subject to a legal challenge in the High Court of Justiciary. In *H.M. Advocate v. Dickson*[82] the seven day notice period was challenged as being contrary to Article 6 of the European Convention of Human Rights. Neither party had given notice that a devolution issue would be raised in the course of the proceedings but during the trial the prosecutor tried to use evidence in the form of a transcript of an interview between the accused and customs officials. During the interview the accused had not been represented by a solicitor and sought to challenge use of the evidence arguing that her right to a fair trial had been prejudiced. The Crown argued that the devolution issue could not be taken since it had not been notified. Counsel for the accused responded that the seven day limit violated the right "to have adequate time and facilities for the preparation" of the defence case. The High Court held that the seven

---

[81] The relevant authority means the relevant law officers—the Lord Advocate and the Advocate General.

[82] 1999 SCCR 859 discussed in C. Gane in note 11.

day limit did not infringe this right "given the need to operate effective and expeditious time-tables in criminal proceedings" and that the time limit could be varied by the court if the interests of justice so demand. Gane comments that whilst this may be the case in relation to proceedings on indictment, there may be a problem in summary proceedings. He argues that the requirement for the accused to notify a devolution issue before he/she is called upon to plead means that "typically, where they appear from custody following an arrest the night before, they probably will have had only a brief conversation with their legal adviser (if any) and effectively less than a morning to identify and formulate the devolution issue".

Proceedings in England and Wales

(A) Devolution References

It is mandatory that a tribunal from which there is no appeal should refer a devolution issue to the Court of Appeal and any other tribunal may make such a reference.[83] A magistrates' court may make a reference to the High Court.[84] Where a devolution issue arises in civil proceedings in other courts, the lower court may refer the matter to the Court of Appeal except in the case of the magistrates' court or the House of Lords.[85] The High Court may not refer a matter to the Court of Appeal if the devolution issue arises in proceedings referred to it from a magistrates' court. Where a devolution issue arises in proceedings before the Court of Appeal, except where the issue has been referred to it by a lower court, the Court of Appeal may refer the matter to the Judicial Committee of the Privy Council.[86]

In criminal proceedings a lower court may refer a devolution issue to the High Court (summary proceedings) or the Court of Appeal (proceedings on indictment).[87] The Court of Appeal may refer a

---

[83] Scotland Act 1998 Sched. 6, Part II, para. 20, Government of Wales Act Sched. 8, Part II para. 8, Northern Ireland Act Sched. 10, Part III, para. 17.
[84] Scotland Act 1998 Sched. 6, Part II, para. 18, Government of Wales Act Sched. 8, Part II para. 6, Northern Ireland Act Sched. 10, Part III, para. 15.
[85] Scotland Act 1998 Sched. 6, Part II, para. 19(2)(b), Government of Wales Act Sched. 8, Part II para. 7, Northern Ireland Act Sched. 10, Part III, para. 16.
[86] Scotland Act 1998 Sched. 6, Part II, para. 22, Government of Wales Act Sched. 8, Part II para. 10, Northern Ireland Act Sched. 10, Part III, para. 19.
[87] Scotland Act 1998 Sched. 6, Part II, para. 21, Government of Wales Act Sched. 8, Part II para. 9, Northern Ireland Act Sched. 10, Part III, para. 18.

devolution issue to the Judicial Committee of the Privy Council except where a devolution reference has been made to it by a lower court.[88]

(B) APPEALS

An appeal against a determination of a devolution issue by the High Court or the Court of Appeal on a reference from a lower court lies to the Judicial Committee of the Privy Council. Leave to appeal is required but special leave can be granted by the Judicial Committee where it is refused by the court itself.[89]

Proceedings in cases where devolution issues are raised are governed by the Practice Direction, Devolution Issues (and Crown Office Applications in Wales), adopted in July 1999.[90] The Practice Direction specifically relates to proceedings in which a devolution issue under the Government of Wales Act is raised in courts in England and Wales. However, should devolution issues arise under the Scotland Act or the Northern Ireland Act, the Practice Direction is to be adapted as required. It applies to proceedings in England and Wales in the Magistrates' Courts, the county courts, the Crown Court, the High Court and the Court of Appeal (Civil and Criminal Divisions).

The Practice Direction makes clear that any party to the proceedings may raise a devolution issue but a court may also require that a devolution issue be considered even if the parties have failed to specify that a devolution issue arises. If the court does so determine "it must state what that devolution is clearly and concisely".

The court must ensure that a devolution order is sent to the Attorney General and the National Assembly for Wales except if the court is receiving a reference from a lower court. Normally the lower court would have required such an order. The receiving court need only notify a devolution issue if it determines the existence of a new devolution issue not previously identified. The Attorney General and the National Assembly for Wales have fourteen days in which to

---

[88] Scotland Act 1998 Sched. 6, Part II, para. 22, Government of Wales Act Sched. 8, Part II para. 10, Northern Ireland Act Sched. 10, Part III, para. 19.

[89] Scotland Act 1998 Sched. 6, Part II, para. 23. Government of Wales Act Sched. 8, Part II para. 11, Northern Ireland Act Sched. 10, Part III, para. 20.

[90] Civil Procedure Rules, July 1999 [1999] 3 All E.R. 466; [1999] 1 W.L.R. 1592; [1999] 2 Cr. App. Rep. 486.

notify the court that he/she/it wishes to take part as a party in proceedings. In exceptional circumstances the court may order that this period be extended. If the Attorney General or the National Assembly for Wales wishes to require the court to refer the matter to the Judicial Committee, a notice must be sent to the court "as soon as practicable".

The Practice Direction, unlike the Scottish legislation, lays down the factors to be taken into consideration by a court in exercising its discretion as to whether to make a reference. These are listed in rule 9 as follows:

- the importance of the devolution issue to the public in general and to the parties to the proceedings

- whether the reference will be decisive of the matters in dispute

- whether all the relevant findings of fact have been made

- the additional delay and costs that would be incurred in making a reference.

These factors are very similar to the factors identified by the Master of the Rolls in the Stock Exchange Case[91] in discussing references to the European Court of Justice. In that case the Master of the Rolls in effect directed courts in England and Wales to consider three important factors before a reference is made. The court must establish the facts, it must decide whether a ruling by the Court of Justice would be critical in deciding the case and it must decide whether it can, with confidence, interpret the relevant provision of Community law. The Practice Direction differs only in the recognition that there may be a significant public interest in the outcome of a case. The clear similarity is the distinction between fact finding and legal interpretation drawn in the two types of reference procedures. The referring court is the master of the facts and the receiving court is the master of the law.

The form of reference is as provided in the Judicial Committee (Devolution Issues) Rules discussed above. Where the reference is to another superior court, the Practice Direction lays down the information to be provided. The requirements are in the same terms as in the Scottish Acts of Sederunt and Adjournal.

---

[91] [1993] 1 All E.R. 420.

There is, of course, no distinction between the Welsh and English legal orders and the courts form part of the same court structure. However, there is a practical consideration that distinguishes the courts in Wales and that is the right of parties to use the Welsh language. As Roddick has stated, litigants are "likely in the future to want to make increasing use of the Welsh language in the courts, particularly in cases involving the operation of the Welsh Assembly".[92] In recognition of this fact, the Practice Direction makes two important provisions to overcome any likely difficulties. Rule 12 recognises that parties might want to raise linguistic problems in the comparison of the Welsh and English texts of Assembly subordinate legislation. Bearing in mind that all Welsh subordinate legislation will be made in English and Welsh and both versions have equal standing,[93] linguistic problems may well become legal issues. The Practice Direction allows courts in these circumstances to appoint a Welsh speaking judicial assessor to assist the court.

The second provision is in relation to proceedings for judicial review. "It would have seemed very odd if disputes between citizens and the National Assembly for Wales relating to purely Welsh affairs had inevitably to be commenced and heard exclusively in England".[94] Rules 13 and 14 allows for the transfer of judicial review cases involving devolution issues or issues concerning the National Assembly, the Welsh Executive or any Welsh public body even if the cases do not involve a devolution issue to be transferred to the Law Courts in Cardiff. As Roddick points out, this will facilitate the hearing of these particular public law cases in Welsh. It also raises the interesting speculative question as to whether it will also lead to an increasing divergence between principles of judicial review as they are applied in Wales and as they are applied in England.

An attempt has been made to raise a devolution issue in relation to the use of the Welsh language in proceedings in the Employment Appeal Tribunal. The Court of Appeal (Civil Division) held, however, that the legislation did not require the EAT to hear cases in the Welsh language and no devolution issue arose.[95]

The Practice Direction provides that devolution issues should be raised at an early stage in the proceedings although specific time

---

[92] W. Roddick, in note 58 above.
[93] Government of Wales Act s.122.
[94] Roddick, n. 51 above.
[95] *Williams v. Cowell and another* [2000] W.L.R. 187.

limits are not provided. In civil proceedings in county courts and the High Court a devolution issue must be raised in the claim form or in the defence. The court can, however, allow a devolution issue to be raised in the course of proceedings. In criminal proceedings in the Crown Court a defendant must raise a devolution issue at the Plea and Directions hearing. There appears to be no provision in this case for the court to allow a devolution issue to be raised in the course of proceedings. If this is the case, then there may be a breach of Article 6 of the European Convention, a point which could be taken on appeal to the Court of Appeal or on a reference to the Judicial Committee if required by the Assembly or the Attorney General. In criminal proceedings in the Magistrates' Court the devolution issue must be raised after the defendant has been charged. On appeal to the Court of Appeal the devolution issue must be specified in the application notice and cannot subsequently be raised without the permission of the court.

Proceedings in Northern Ireland

(A) DEVOLUTION REFERENCES

It is mandatory that a tribunal from which there is no appeal must refer a devolution issue to the Court of Appeal in Northern Ireland and any other tribunal may make such a reference.[96] A lower court in Northern Ireland may refer any devolution issue, whether arising in civil or criminal proceedings, to the Court of Appeal in Northern Ireland.[97] The Court of Appeal in Northern Ireland may refer a devolution issue, except where the devolution issue has been referred to it, to the Judicial Committee of the Privy Council.[98]

(B) APPEALS

An appeal against a determination of a devolution issue by the Court of Appeal on a reference from a lower court in Northern Ireland lies

---

[96] Scotland Act 1998 Sched. 6, Part II, para. 29, Government of Wales Act Sched. 8, Part IV para. 26, Northern Ireland Act Sched. 10, Part II, para. 8.
[97] Scotland Act 1998 Sched. 6, Part II, para. 28, Government of Wales Act Sched. 8, Part IV para. 25, Northern Ireland Act Sched. 10, Part II, para. 7.
[98] Scotland Act 1998 Sched. 6, Part II, para. 30, Government of Wales Act Sched. 8, Part IV para. 27, Northern Ireland Act Sched. 10, Part II, para. 9.

to the Judicial Committee. Leave to appeal is necessary but special leave may be granted by the Judicial Committee where leave to appeal is refused.[99]

At the time of writing there is no equivalent Practice Direction for Northern Ireland. It is likely that the Practice Direction for England and Wales will form the basis for the Northern Irish rules.

Proceedings in the House of Lords

Where a devolution issue arises in proceedings in the House of Lords, it shall refer the issue to the Judicial Committee unless the House of Lords deems it more appropriate to deal with the matter itself.[1]

The Judicial Committee of the Privy Council

The three devolution settlements all point to the Judicial Committee of the Privy Council as being the ultimate devolution court. This is not to say that the Judicial Committee will be involved in hearing a significant number of cases. Devolution issues may well be settled in several different courts and may never reach the Judicial Committee. However, there is the potential for a large number of devolution cases reaching the Judicial Committee if only because the number of pathways that are available:

- the relevant Law Officers may refer a Bill or any of its provisions to determine if it is within the legislative competence of the devolved institution

- the law officers and, where relevant, the National Assembly for Wales may require a court to refer any devolution issue to the Judicial Committee in proceedings in which any one of them is a party

- courts may refer devolution issues to the Judicial Committee

---

[99] Scotland Act 1998 Sched. 6, Part II, para. 31, Government of Wales Act Sched. 8, Part IV para. 28, Northern Ireland Act Sched. 10, Part II, para. 10.
[1] Scotland Act 1998 Sched. 6, Part V, para. 32, Government of Wales Act Sched. 8, Part V para. 29, Northern Ireland Act Sched. 10, Part V, para. 32.

- the Judicial Committee is the appeal court from the superior courts where a determination of a devolution issue has been made

- the House of Lords may determine that the Judicial Committee is the more appropriate forum for hearing a case brought to it.

From this brief summary it can be seen that the Judicial Committee may, in fact, be inundated with cases. Conversely it may never be brought into play in the consideration of devolution issues despite the priority that appears to be accorded it in the devolution legislation. "Local" courts may prefer to deal with devolution issues themselves and lower courts in a particular jurisdiction might prefer a reference to a superior "local" court. The law officers might find that a reference is not needed, preferring to leave issues to be dealt with if and when they arise. The appeal procedure depends always on the desire of the parties concerned to go to the ultimate court of appeal. Devolution issues therefore may well be settled in different ways depending on the discretion of a variety of legal personnel. This is despite the fact that Lord Sewel stated during the course of the passage of the Scotland Act that the government had chosen the Judicial Committee as the ultimate devolution court "to minimise the risk of contradictory decisions and to provide an ultimate common court of appeal".[2] Furthermore, Lord Hardie, in debating the power of the Law Officers to require a court to refer a devolution issue stated that "this is to provide a fast-track procedure" to ensure that a devolution issue must be referred to the Judicial Committee "to ensure consistency of decisions".

There is, of course, an inherent tension in providing for a centralised court within a devolution settlement and these issues do not appear to have been fully resolved. In Scotland, it is anticipated that most devolution issues will be settled within the Scottish legal order and, as the Counsel General for Wales has stated, the move to hear Welsh judicial review cases in Wales is a recognition of the need for judicial devolution. At the European level, this tension is eased by leaving intact the appellate jurisdiction within the Member States and by endowing the European Court of Justice with an interpretative function only. The ECJ is not an appeal court, final decision rests within the Member States. The devolution reference procedure

---

[2] H.L Deb vol 593 col 579 October, 8 1998.

mirrors this possibility but the Judicial Committee has the dual role of receiving references and as acting as a court of appeal in other cases. It may be difficult therefore for the Judicial Committee to attempt to establish the kind of dialogue between it and the courts in the United Kingdom regions that has been established, albeit within a delicate balance, between the ECJ and the courts of the Member States.

Furthermore, giving a Law Officer, a political appointee and member of the executive branch of government, the right to require a court to refer a matter to the Judicial Committee may well create tensions. Direct and legally sanctioned political interference in the judicial process is an unusual constitutional development seen before only under the Government of Northern Ireland Act. Whereas Lord Hardie may see this as a way of getting a speedy response to a devolution issue, the local court might as easily see it as interfering with the proper operation and conduct of the courts. This will particularly be the case if the law officers use the power to require a reference widely and without due regard to the need to respect the integrity and independence of the courts. In order to respect this independence, the Law Officers might opt to use their powers sparingly.

In the course of time these tensions may be alleviated or prove to be non-existent but, in the short term, they are exacerbated by the fact that the Judicial Committee is an unknown, untried and untested devolution court. Lord Steel, in debate, stated that "it is entirely unsatisfactory that the whole of the part of this Bill (the Scotland Bill) should be put on appeal to something that is amorphous and ill-defined".[3] His fears were echoed by Lord Hope who stated that "a particular point of concern is that the Scottish judiciary should be properly represented".[4]

It is, of course, a truism that any court, whether newly created or an existing court, that is given ultimate control over devolution issues would be unknown, untried and untested. In this sense, Boyd's argument that disputes over competencies should be settled by a judicial body in which all the parties should have confidence can only be tested in retrospect.

The most thorough debate on the choice of the appropriate judicial forum for the resolution of devolution issues took place almost at the

---

[3] H.L Deb vol 593 col 580 October 8, 1998.
[4] In the same debate.

last moment in the House of Lords' debate on the Scotland Bill.[5] The debate was on an amendment that reference to the judicial committee should be replaced by a reference to a constitutional court with an additional schedule setting out proposals for an appointing committee to the court. A further amendment would have removed the possibility of the Lord Chancellor and former Lord Chancellors being involved in the court.

In effect three options had been open to the drafters of the devolution legislation. The final court of appeal and reference on devolution issues could be:

- the House of Lords
- the Judicial Committee
- a new judicial body.

It could be argued that the House of Lords would have been the most appropriate body to deal with devolution issues. It certainly meets Boyd's criteria of having the confidence of potential parties to disputes. The House of Lords is a well known and familiar institution with a high degree of expertise in deciding difficult constitutional cases in unfamiliar terrain. Cases arising out of United Kingdom membership of the E.U. being undoubtedly the most difficult constitutional issues to have faced the courts in the last half century. However, the House of Lords does not have jurisdiction to hear appeals from the Scottish High Court of Justiciary for the sound reason that the Scottish Parliament at the time of the Acts of Union did not itself have jurisdiction to hear criminal appeals and could not therefore transfer a jurisdiction it did not possess to the House of Lords. Many devolution issues have already arisen in Scottish criminal courts and many more are likely to arise. To create a way of appeal on these devolution questions to the House of Lords would have occasioned major criticism and opposition within Scotland.

The only alternative existing judicial forum is the Judicial Committee. It cannot be said that this body has either the prestige or the visibility of the House of Lords despite the fact that, in practice, the Judicial Committee and the appellate committee of the House of Lords are chosen from the same panel of judges and are, in fact,

---

[5] H.L Deb vol 593 cols 1963–1986 October 28, 1998.

twins. As Lord Clyde pointed out in debate, the 12 Law Lords sit in committees of five, four days per week. Five judges sit in the Judicial Committee and the other five as the appellate committee of the House of Lords.[6] However it was clear in the debate that the Judicial Committee was seen as an amorphous and unwieldy institution, whatever the practical realities as explained by Lord Clyde.

Lord Lester, one of the proposers of the amendment, was opposed to the use of the Judicial Committee as a devolution court for three reasons. He argued that the Judicial Committee is too large and amorphous, dominated by retired English judges from the English Court of Appeal. Its membership, he stated, is "large and uneven, and geographically completely unbalanced". His second argument was based on the lack of transparency in the way a panel is appointed. In theory the Lord Chancellor, but in practice the senior Law Lord, decides on the composition of the panel but he/she has no criteria on which to judge the suitability of a particular judge. For example, there is no requirement that a person has expertise in questions of public law or human rights. Finally, Lord Lester argued that the use of the Judicial Committee was a breach of the principle of separation of powers and institutional independence because of the particular role of the Lord Chancellor. The Lord Chancellor is entitled to sit as part of the Judicial Committee (or House of Lords), a situation which may to lead him/her deciding cases brought by the Attorney General on behalf of the United Kingdom government of which both the Attorney General and Lord Chancellor are members. For these reasons, he argued, the Judicial Committee should be replaced by a constitutional court.

By contrast to the reasoned approach outlined above, arguments in favour of the Judicial Committee tend to be pragmatic. First of all, the Judicial Committee is there. It was established in the nineteenth century to deal with constitutional and political issues arising from the colonies. Indeed Lord Selkirk praised its nineteenth century wealth of expertise.[7] It has more recent expertise dealing with matters arising from the Commonwealth. Furthermore, the Judicial Committee, despite the inter-changeability of personnel is not the House of Lords and the problem of Scottish criminal appeals discussed above is avoided. Furthermore, the Judicial Committee was also the

---

[6] H.L Deb vol 593 col. 1980 October 28, 1998.
[7] H.L Deb vol 593 col. 1963 October 28, 1998.

court entrusted to deal with devolution issues under the Government of Ireland Act 1920 although it was used only once to resolve a devolution issue.

The Lord Chancellor's contribution to the debate was limited. He did not accept the need for a geographical balance in the court dealing with devolution issues. At the same time he accepted that a convention "probably" would develop that in cases arising under the Scotland Act there would be at least one Scottish judge on the panel. He also rejected any moves to withdraw his own discretion as to whether or not to sit in any a particular case. He stated that he would exercise his discretion not to sit where he considered it "inappropriate to do so". Furthermore, he added "I do not accept that there is a category of case . . . to be called constitutional which should be out of bounds of the Lord Chancellor when he sits at the head of the judiciary".[8]

Conclusions

It is worth recalling Boyd's four principles in relation to the resolution of devolution issues. He argued for a system that was limited to questions of vires, that disputes should be settled by a judicial body, that parties should have confidence in that body and that the system chosen should be as speedy and efficient as possible. The first two of these principles have been written into the devolution legislation. However the third and fourth have still to be tested. The idea behind the legislation was obviously that there should be a fast track to the Judicial Committee for the resolution of devolution issues. To date that mechanism has not been used. Devolution issues have arisen but they have been dealt with "locally". This is because cases have typically concerned the relationship between the devolved institutions, in particular the Scottish Executive, and the Human Rights Act. Boyd could not have foreseen that the Human Rights Act would have been passed at the same time as devolution occurred and could not have foreseen the difficulties that the human rights legislation could cause. The Human Rights Act requires judges to apply its provisions and it is likely that most cases where devolution and human rights issues overlap will be dealt with locally.

---

[8] H.L Deb vol 593 col 1984 October 28, 1998.

Given that the Judicial Committee has no experience of dealing with devolution issues it is too early to state whether it will be a speedy and efficient mechanism for the resolution of disputes and whether it will prove to be worthy of the name of a constitutional court. It is also too early to predict how cases will be resolved and what constitutional principles will be adopted. There is a strong argument that the Judicial Committee should be outward and forward looking in its approach if it is to provide a "modern" constitutional framework. In earlier chapters it was argued that the principles of subsidiarity, close co-operation, proportionality and minimum legislation could usefully be borrowed from Europe. European concepts are part and parcel of United Kingdom law and are not unfamiliar to the judiciary. It would seem a logical step to use concepts that are already to hand in the development of our constitutional rules, particularly since the United Kingdom as a Member State of the European Union, has had a role in developing these principles.

One of the issues that has been high-lighted in this chapter is the differences between the devolution settlements in relation to both procedures and in relation to the legal actors involved in the judicial settlement of disputes. In terms of procedures in the various courts, these differences are marginal and merely reflect the existing differences between the legal systems of England and Wales, Scotland, and Northern Ireland. In terms of personnel, however, the legislation has brought to light very real differences in approach. Devolution has imposed new duties on some existing law officers, notably the Lord Advocate and the Attorney General, but in doing so it has pointed to the absence of any functionally equivalent law officer in Northern Ireland and in Wales. Here a solution has been adopted specifically in response to local problems.

Devolution has also brought into sharp relief a clear problem in Scotland relating to the separation of powers. The multiple roles of the Lord Advocate have created problems under the Human Rights Act and lead inevitably to the question of what exactly is the function of the law officer in a modern constitutional order. That question goes beyond the scope of this book but problems under the devolution settlements do suggest that any study of the law officers needs to consider the implications of devolution on their functions.

Chapter 7

The Future of Devolution?

Students of European Community law have become accustomed to thinking in terms of process or stages when they approach their subject. The development of the European legal order has taken place against the background of a debate on the nature of the European enterprise. What kind of Europe is being created? What is meant by the ever closer union? Does a revision of the treaty deepen or widen the process of European integration? Is subsidiarity a federalising principle? Can economic integration progress without political integration? What role do the institutions have in this process? Is the European Court a constitutional court? The questions about the nature of the process of European integration are stated and restated constantly.

Devolution is also a process and, just as was the case with the process of European integration, it is impossible to foresee the direction it will take. It would have been a brave person in 1951, when the Treaty establishing the European Coal and Steel Community was signed, who would have predicted the existence of a single currency fifty years later. In the same way it is difficult to predict where the process of devolution will end. However, it is possible to draw some conclusions about the kind of issues that have emerged already within the scheme of devolution to predict, albeit tentatively, the kind of ongoing issues that will fall to be resolved in the coming years.

This chapter examines factors specific to each of the devolution settlements in turn and then raises questions about the overall structure of United Kingdom constitutional law arising from the process of devolution. The chapter is structured in terms of an analysis of the stability and robustness of the framework of devolution and of its logic.

Scotland

It is probably true to say that the Scottish Parliament, in whatever form it may take in the future, is now a permanent feature of the Scottish constitutional landscape. It is unthinkable that there will not be a Scottish Parliament. However, the place of the Scottish Parliament in the United Kingdom constitutional landscape is not fully determined.

A substantial minority of MSPs and of the Scottish population as a whole is in favour of independence from the United Kingdom. Over the last few years support for independence has never risen above about thirty to forty per cent of the population and support has often depended on the charisma of individual leaders. Nonetheless there is a persistent demand for home rule in the sense of the re-creation of the Scottish state as an independent nation state. Thus when Winnie Ewing MSP as the oldest member of the Parliament took the Chair at the first session and announced the resumption of the Scottish Parliament she was clearly making a political statement about the nature of the Parliament.[1] It cannot be ruled out therefore that the Scottish Parliament is but a stepping stone to independence, provided always that the SNP can demonstrate sufficient support in the elections to the Scottish Parliament to use the Parliament as the means of attaining independence. This will be difficult given the electoral system outlined in Chapter 2. Furthermore, the legislation itself does not recognise the legitimacy of the claim to withdraw from the United Kingdom. In this respect it differs from the Northern Ireland Act where the need for ongoing consent to remain part of the United Kingdom is built into the settlement. Thus the transformation of the present Scottish Parliament into the parliament of an independent Scottish state would seem to depend on at least two factors. The first is sufficient electoral support for an independence party and then the withdrawal of Scotland from the union. It is not impossible to envisage such steps but unlikely without a significant switch in voter preferences in Scotland.

At least for the immediately foreseeable future therefore it is likely that the Scottish Parliament will remain as a devolved institution

---

[1] "I want to begin with the words that I have always wanted to say or to hear someone else saying: the Scottish Parliament, which adjourned on 25 March 1707 is hereby reconvened" Scottish Parliament Official Report Vol. 1 No. 1 May 12, 1999 col. 5.

within the United Kingdom. However, some of the limitations imposed on the Parliament will have to be revisited. The need to revisit the devolution settlement will arise because of a popular misunderstanding of it. It is clearly the case in Scotland that the Scottish Parliament and the Scottish Executive have quickly become the focus of political debate. It is true that much of the debate in the press in Scotland has been negative.[2] By comparison there has been no debate at all about issues relating to Scotland that are dealt with in Westminster. People in Scotland believe that the Scottish Parliament deals with all issues relating to Scotland and clearly do not appreciate the niceties of the Scotland Act in relation to reserved matters and devolved matters.

European lawyers are familiar with the complaint that European law is too technical and distant to allow a proper understanding of it by the citizens of Europe. To some extent the blame has fallen on experts for refusing to share their knowledge. Mattera for example, argued that knowledge of European law "ne peut pas rester la prérogative d'un petit nombre de specialistes, technocrates et professeurs de l'université, qui en revendiqueraient l'exclusivité avec complaisance et cupidité, sortes de vestales gardant le feu sacré".[3] This argument can be applied too to the Scottish devolution settlement because it is only by a firm understanding of the Scotland Act that a citizen could understand the extent or limitations of the powers of the newly created institutions. Devolution is intended to bring the citizen closer to the institutions of government but to do so clarity is required in explicating the full extent of the devolution settlement. Explanation is needed to the public as to why some matters are devolved and others are not. Simplification of the legislation with a reduction in the extensive lists of reserved matters would assist.

In explaining their roles and functions to the people of Scotland, Scottish parliamentarians will also be able to define for themselves the purpose of the Parliament. At this point that purpose is not fully clarified. One effect of devolution has been to enlarge the size and power of the Scottish Executive, formerly known as the Scottish Office. The elections to the Parliament endowed the Scottish Executive with a direct legitimacy that may have been lacking in the

---

[2] I. MacWhirter, "Scotland year Zero: The First Year at Holyrood" in G. Hassan and C. Warhurst (eds.) *The New Scottish Politics* (The Stationery Office, 2000).
[3] A. Mattera, *Le Marché Unique Européen,* (Paris, Jupiler, 1990).

past. Devolution was meant to do more than this. It was meant to create a relationship between executive and parliament that did not exist between Whitehall and Westminster and the Scottish Office and Westminster. A local parliament would introduce transparency and openness in decision taking and create a new politics. The executive was to be subject to the tightest of scrutiny making accountability issues central to the new politics.

To date the Scottish Parliament has not fully met these challenges. The Scottish Executive in many ways acts as if it were a United Kingdom cabinet and does not appear to have entered into any kind of partnership or dialogue with the Parliament or its committees. Indeed it seems in many ways that the Executive has gone out of its way to borrow traditions from Westminster that are unsuitable for modern inclusive politics. The reliance on the doctrine of collective ministerial responsibility or the limitations accepted by Ministers on the right to information in the Code of Practice for Scottish Ministers are examples of the way in which the Scottish Executive has continued the "old" politics of Westminster and Whitehall. Pyper recalls Donald Dewar's intervention in "the fray" between the committees and some members of the Scottish Executive. He states that "Dewar criticised the committees developing practice of routinely calling the Ministers before them."[4] In its planning for the Scottish Parliament, the Consultative Steering Group had not envisaged such a fray but a power sharing arrangement between expert committees and the Scottish Executive. There is little evidence to date of such genuine power sharing.

The committees of the Scottish Parliament have yet fully to assert their true weight since the members of these committees are still feeling their way through both procedural and substantive issues. Members of the committees do not have the full range of support that is available to Scottish Ministers and the Parliament is understaffed in comparison with the Scottish Administration. Civic society in Scotland has not yet turned its attention to the committees as a central lobbying point relying on an older and established web of contacts within the Executive. All this was to be expected. The Parliament is not a year old yet and its members are on a steep learning curve. Many of the members have come from local

---

[4] R. Pyper, "The First Minister and the Scottish Executive" in G. Hassan and C. Warhurst in note 2.

government and some from Westminster. They have to unlearn traditions and procedures as well as to embrace new ones. Furthermore, the first Scottish Parliament was elected mid-term of the existing United Kingdom executive. The Labour Party had established its priorities as part of a United Kingdom programme rather than with a specific eye for a programme of Scottish government. For the next election each party will need to have a rather more Scottish focussed programme.

An additional complicating feature of devolution in Scotland has been the decision to apply the provisions of the Human Rights Act to measures taken by the Scottish Executive. As explained in Chapter 6, the Lord Advocate who now has a number of overlapping and possibly conflicting roles, is head of the system of criminal prosecution in Scotland. He/she also has a role in the appointment of judges. Both aspects of the post have been subject to challenge in the courts and at times it appeared that the Scottish Executive collectively was being attacked simultaneously in the courts and in the press. The resignation of Lord Hardie as Lord Advocate did little to support the apparently beleagured Scottish Executive. The involvement of the law officers in the more political/legal/constitutional issues arising from the devolution settlement and from the introduction of the Human Rights Act does provide the opportunity for a review of the role of the law officers. This is an issue that is likely to be revisited in the coming years. In particular, in the context of Scotland where a Ministry of Justice has been created, there seems little need for the presence of a law officer per se within the Parliament. The Welsh example, if it is becomes a successful model, may show that legal advice to the Executive can be provided from external sources and does not require a political appointee within the structure of government itself.

Wales

Support for devolution in Wales was ambivalent and there is no way, short of devolution becoming an election issue, of measuring whether that support has changed. Ambivalent commitment to devolution plus the absence of a well defined Welsh pro devolution political culture, as there is in Scotland, led to the adoption of a devolution settlement that is rather ambiguous. This suggests the need for several issues to be revisited.

One key problem is the very structure of the National Assembly for Wales. The Assembly is the executive branch of government in Wales. The Assembly Cabinet is, in law, a committee of the Assembly. Assembly Secretaries are AMs having delegated powers. This structure is based on a compromise between a local government structure and the system of cabinet government used elsewhere in the United Kingdom. Structurally this is an unstable settlement. The lack of fit between this system and other forms of government structures within the United Kingdom is already apparent in the arrangements that have been adopted to co-ordinate policy within the United Kingdom discussed in Chapter 5. The Memorandum of Understanding and the concordats adopt the legal fiction that the Assembly Cabinet is the Executive branch of government for Wales in the same way as the Scottish Executive and the Northern Ireland Executive are within their respective jurisdictions. This is the first recognition that the system of devolution is just too asymmetrical to function in a co-ordinated way.

However, the structural problem cannot be resolved without attention to the question of functions. It has been stressed in this book that the National Assembly for Wales does not have powers to adopt primary legislation. The traditional distinction between legislative and executive functions in this context becomes irrelevant. Without the power to adopt primary legislation, the Assembly lacks a central focus. In Wales there is the anomaly that an Assembly deriving its legitimacy from the will of the people demonstrated in elections lacks the power to carry out the functions associated elsewhere within the United Kingdom with such a body. The National Assembly for Wales therefore has legitimacy but lacks a functional capacity proper to its status whereas prior to devolution the Welsh Office had an extensive functional capacity yet lacked legitimacy. The whole point of devolution was to rectify this position. It has merely turned it upside down.

Again there are lessons to be learned from the United Kingdom experience in Europe. The first direct elections to the European Parliament (initially tagged an Assembly by the Treaty of Rome) took place in 1979. From that date on the European Parliament has struggled to assert its right to play an increased role in the legislative process at the level of the European Union. From having a merely consultative role in the legislative process, the European Parliament has moved from a co-operation procedure towards a co-decision procedure that brings it into the heart of the legislative process at the

European level. Whilst there is still much more scope for the involvement of the European Parliament the lesson is none the less clear. A body deriving its legitimacy from the electoral process should not be excluded from the legislative process and its role should not be limited to consultation.

The question of whether the National Assembly for Wales should have legislative power is one that will arise in the future. Perhaps this is not an immediate issue but as the Assembly becomes bedded down, as the devolution process begins to bite elsewhere, then an Assembly without a purpose will inevitably seek one. Before this can happen a pro devolution political culture focussing on Welsh issues is needed and a refocussing of Welsh politicians towards Wales. The creation of the Assembly itself, the shift in emphasis in the courts towards hearing cases in Wales and perhaps in the Welsh language, and the second round of elections may be factors to be considered in assessing how far that political culture has developed. Perhaps the key issue is whether the Labour Party can resolve its own differences over devolution. If it does not and Plaid Cymru win a greater share of the seats in the Assembly the pressure towards a stronger devolution settlement would seem almost inevitable. Cohabitation between Plaid Cymru in Cardiff and Labour in London seems unlikely to be a successful combination given the "dependency" relationship of the Welsh Assembly on Westminster for primary legislation.

Northern Ireland

To date the most striking feature about devolution to Northern Ireland has been, of course, the difficulties surrounding it. The political situation in Northern Ireland is unique and it is not possible to use the lessons from either Scotland or Wales to apply them to Northern Ireland where devolution is a part of a wide and ambitious peace making process. The creation of institutions, their suspension and restoration demonstrates the very fragility of devolution in Northern Ireland.

The Belfast Agreement, achieved on Good Friday 1998, was a delicate compromise between two competing positions and traditions. It was an attempt to reconcile the desire of Republicans to achieve a united Ireland and the desire of Unionists to remain part of the United Kingdom. The Belfast Agreement was supported by the governments of Ireland and the United Kingdom jointly and was supported by the European Union. The President of the United States, Bill Clinton, and his administration invested time and energy into achieving the compromise. By definition, success was never guaranteed.

Devolution, of course, is not new to Northern Ireland. Apart from this recent experience, Northern Ireland was governed under a devolved process for 50 years. That experiment failed because it did not engage the loyalties and the support of the Catholic population. It was based on majoritarian politics, which had the effect of excluding the Catholic community from the political process. The civil rights movement brought to light the failings within the system and direct rule had to be re-imposed. The 1998 Agreement attempted to legislate for parity of esteem and for equality issues—the very issues that had been neglected in the first devolution attempt. Therefore it was based on a model unknown elsewhere within the United Kingdom of a pre-determined scheme of inclusion. In Wales and Scotland devolution was to herald inclusiveness and a new politics and the electoral scheme does prevent land-slide majoritarianism. However, there was never an attempt to impose political balance by guaranteeing the need for cross community support in both the adoption of policy in some areas and in the choice of the Executive. Although the d'Hondt formula has been used for the selection of chairs and vice-chairs of the committees in Wales and Scotland its use is not mandatory. Neither has it been used to choose the Scottish Ministers and the Assembly Secretaries. In Northern Ireland it has imposed proportional representation in all aspects of the work of the new institutions. Political balance is even required at the very head of government where the unique feature of First Minister and Deputy First Minister limits the power of the head of government to direct policy.

Devolution to Northern Ireland is therefore much more precise and formulaic, the Secretary of State for Northern Ireland having a much greater level of involvement than that accorded to his/her territorial equivalents elsewhere. Each part of the process was governed by an attempt to create consensus. Devolution may be the best compromise in dealing with the seemingly intractable problems of Northern Ireland. However, it may be an insufficiently robust compromise to meet all the conflicting demands that are placed on the political and legal process of devolution. At the end of the day extremely hard political choices may have to be faced—either the withdrawal of Great Britain from the entire space of Irish politics or the rejection of Republican demands for parity of esteem within the British State. Both choices are unpalatable. The latter has been tried and led to resort to the violence that is currently the occasion for the rejection of devolution by the Unionist community. The former would violate the principle of consent unless that consent could be obtained by force of persuasion and argument. If devolution does not work then these choices must at least be discussed.

The United or Union Kingdom

The process of devolution has called into question the very nature of the United Kingdom in the same way that membership of the European Union opened the debate about the nature of the nation state and the nature of political and legal sovereignty. Membership of the European Union involved the United Kingdom in a close web of relations with other European states and necessitated interaction with institutions of government at the European level. The site of authority shifted in some matters away from the United Kingdom acting independently towards the United Kingdom acting jointly or severally with other members of the European Union. Devolution is like a mirror image of this process and many of the issues confronted in the twentieth century in relation to United Kingdom membership of the European Union will have to be settled in the twenty-first in relation to devolution.

Devolution is the recognition in law of the national identities and national boundaries that exist inside the nation state that happens to be called the United Kingdom, but which could easily fall into a definition of a union kingdom. For some citizens of the United Kingdom it creates an additional layer of government between central government and local government, *i.e.* regional government. Citizens of the United Kingdom who happen to live in England do not have regional government. Thus the United Kingdom, taken as a whole, is not characterised as having multi-layered government—that description only applies at the moment to Scotland, Northern Ireland and Wales.[5] However, even where devolution has occurred, as this book

---

[5] The creation of a mayor and Assembly in London does not fall into the definition of devolution used in this book. It is however another element in the process of decentralisation and modernisation.

demonstrates, devolution is a differentiated process. Thus the United Kingdom as a whole could be said to have multi-textured government in the sense that the layers of government are uneven throughout. Multi-textured government is the British response chosen to dealing with the union state.

Multi-layered government is a feature of many democratic states. The most common form of multi-layered government is the federal or confederal system. This model has been rejected in the United Kingdom for many reasons, the most obvious being the absence of any fully articulated desire for devolution within England. Other models of multi-layered government exist. In Spain the autonomous regions have a greater or lesser degree of autonomy depending on the strength of the regional government face to face with the Spanish authorities. Even in Spain, where devolution is asymmetrical, all regions of Spain have some degree of home rule or autonomy within an understanding of principles of constitutionality.[6]

Some of the institutions set up after the Belfast Agreement or under the Memorandum of Understanding discussed in Chapter 5 do suggest an almost federal like approach to devolution. However, the Memorandum of Understanding mistakes multi- textured for multi-layered government. The key issue is the position of England in these arrangements. The United Kingdom and England are equated. United Kingdom ministers, for example, represent the interests of England in discussions where matters have been devolved to Scotland. In any federal system, the interests of the regional level of government are treated as distinct from those of the centre. Again there is need to resort to a legal fiction to allow arrangements to operate. This may suggest the need for the creation of separate English ministries in time or other alternative arrangements.

The management of a multi-textured state is a novel constitutional endeavour. There is no model elsewhere in which some regions have autonomy and others not at all, although there are examples of differentiated devolution. Looking to Europe as a model, it could be argued that the concept of flexibility could be used to characterise multi-textured government. At the level of the European Union, flexibility permits some states to move forward towards integration at a different pace than others. Its mirror image may be used to describe the process whereby parts of the United Kingdom achieve devolution

---

[6] C. Villiers, *The Spanish Legal Tradition* (Aldershot: Ashgate, 1999).

at different rates or do not participate in the process at all. Thus until there is a demand for regional government in England, the English regions can opt-out of devolution.

The proposal that multi-textured government can only be managed within the context of a written constitutional order may be over stating the case. In political terms British pragmatism might be sufficient to see through the successful operation of devolution. However, legally binding rules of play are needed whether developed by the courts or the legislature. In most constitutional traditions such rules would indeed be part of a written constitutional order. At the European level constitutional principles such as flexibility have been written into the treaties themselves.

Principles governing intra-governmental and intra-parliamentary relations need to be developed. In particular Westminster needs to accept that the power to legislate in non-reserved areas has been irrevocably transferred to the Scottish Parliament and the Northern Ireland Assembly and, perhaps in the future, to the National Assembly for Wales. In matters of concurrent powers constitutional principles are required governing their exercise. One potential option is to borrow the principle of subsidiarity at least as a test for when and how concurrent power can be exercised. Principles relating to the status of legislation adopted by the devolved parliamentary bodies must also be settled. This book has argued that legislation adopted by the devolved legislatures is primary legislation within the legal order of the devolved jurisdiction. Should Westminster legislate in any devolved area then principles need to be adopted which allow the courts to disapply legislation that conflicts with the devolution settlement. Without such a rule or procedure, the devolution settlement is not secured in law.

The resolution of devolution issues by the courts is another matter that requires to be revisited. The comparison of the three devolution settlements in this respect raises several important questions. The first relates to the roles and functions of the law officers in the modern constitutional order. The devolution settlements have, in the main, bolted on new tasks to existing offices of state. However, the introduction of devolution and a need to comply with human rights principles in Scotland has caused questions to be raised about these overlapping functions. In the debates on the Scotland Bill questions were raised about the role of the Lord Chancellor in a quasi-constitutional court, the Judicial Committee of the Privy Council. The time has therefore come to address the role of the law officers in the new constitutional settlement.

Finally it is clear that a new constitutional language and new constitutional concepts are required to attempt to describe and develop the process of devolution. Throughout this book reference has been made to lessons that can be drawn from membership of the European Union. This is partly the personal preference of a European lawyer but also because of the existing interaction of our constitutional law with European legal concepts. The lessons to be drawn from membership of the European Union are particularly apposite in studying devolution. Certain lessons stand out: the need for principles, the need for the acceptance of clear objectives, the possibility for differentiated or flexible devolution. Most importantly of all, however, is the recognition of devolution as a long-term process requiring positive engagement to achieve equitable solutions to the legitimate demand for home rule.

Index

193